SHIFT

SHIFT

A BLIND MAN'S VISION FOR REWRITING
THE STORIES THAT LIMIT US

RUSSELL REDENBAUGH

NEW YORK

NASHVILLE • MELBOURNE • VANCOUVER

SHIFT
A BLIND MAN'S VISION FOR REWRITING THE STORIES THAT LIMIT US

© 2021 **RUSSELL REDENBAUGH**

Published in New York, New York, by Morgan James Publishing. Morgan James is a trademark of Morgan James, LLC. www.MorganJamesPublishing.com

Morgan James BOGO™

A **FREE** ebook edition is available for you or a friend with the purchase of this print book.

CLEARLY SIGN YOUR NAME ABOVE

Instructions to claim your free ebook edition:
1. Visit MorganJamesBOGO.com
2. Sign your name CLEARLY in the space above
3. Complete the form and submit a photo of this entire page
4. You or your friend can download the ebook to your preferred device

ISBN 978-1-63047-498-0 paperback
ISBN 978-1-63047-738-7 eBook
ISBN 978-1-68350-219-7 hardcover
Library of Congress Control Number: 2016914544

Cover Design by:
Rachel Lopez
www.r2cdesign.com

Morgan James PUBLISHING **Builds** *with...* **Habitat for Humanity®** Peninsula and Greater Williamsburg

Morgan James is a proud partner of Habitat for Humanity Peninsula and Greater Williamsburg. Partners in building since 2006.

Get involved today! Visit MorganJamesPublishing.com/giving-back

CONTENTS

ACKNOWLEDGMENTS

I offer my sincerest thanks:

To my cousin and friend Brent Bingham who taught me how to rock climb.

To Dean Blanchard of Wharton, who gave me a chance to prove I could do the work and be employable, and the Wharton School for making an investment in me that paid off for us both.

To my brother David, my first best friend whom I miss to this day.

To the many family and friends who did not let me give up on myself

To Dr. Fernando Flores, who taught me how to think.

To my Uncle Jake Garn, United States Senator and space shuttle astronaut who visited me in the hospital for forty-two days straight.

To George Gilder, who taught me to listen to technology and how it changes the economy by changing the relative prices of factors of production.

To all the neighbors that day in Salt Lake City who rushed to my aid, especially Ruth Johnson, the nurse who saved my life.

To Dr. Art Laffer, who taught me serious economics.

To Dr. Drew Lebby, my dear friend and trusted advisor for over thirty-five years.

To James McClennen, who gave me the chance to prove I could learn to invest.

To my fraternity brother Kendall Oldroyd who encouraged me during graduate school during what appeared to be a futile job search, with his words, "if you were a stock, I would invest in you."

To Stanford and Harvard for rejecting my graduate school applications. They joined the extensive list who said, "You can't."

FOREWORD
by **George Gilder**

Is your life in need of a shift? Do you feel that you are drifting through your existence, pushed down by forces beyond your control, mired in a meager narrative by the pressure of circumstance, your ceiling capped, your future a dreary repetition of the past?

Do you believe you have free will to change course? Do you believe that your life can be transformed, not merely by small increments but by radical new shifts of direction and resolve?

Many of you think you are beyond such concerns. Many of you already deem yourselves successful. Complacent about your career and accomplishments, you want to cruise forward without rocking any boats or risking any setbacks on the road to a comfortable retirement. But everyone, from our President to a homeless man on the streets, from an investor who diversifies his holdings into mediocrity, to a business executive who hesitates to act in the face of apparent risks, from an unmarried mother mired in the welfare state to a Senator paralyzed by polls and press and precedent, needs to grasp the crucial truths about change and redemption luminously expounded in this book.

"What story is trapping you?" Redenbaugh asks. "What story will free you to move forward? That is the story you need. That is your new narrative."

Most of us are never required to break from the drab drift of mediocrity. Most of us, says Redenbaugh in this guidebook for human achievement, never discover the real dimensions of human possibility. We are creatures of habit and happenstance, drift, and drudgery. We are believers in the imperial privileges of what already exists rather than authors of the narrative of our lives of change.

Many historians, economists, and other experts imagine that America has reached this kind of impasse. We have come to the end of the American frontier and fathomed the limits of the world. With a massive overhang of debt, massive encrustation of laws and rules, looming challenges of aging and disability, "climate change," and overpopulation, our horizons seem to be closing in on us. Compared to previous eras of industrial revolution and creativity, leading government and university economists see a period of "secular stagnation" at hand, an era of dismal stasis and decline, as technology loses its creative dynamism and enterprise faces a disabled destiny.

Dominant in government and the universities, a "cautionary principle"—safety first and foremost—have unleashed regulatory webs of rules that stifle enterprise, invention, and energy production. Climate change allegedly portends a steady shrinkage in the world's population, prosperity, and resources. Diminishing energy supplies doom entrepreneurial initiative and manufacturing expansion. We face a future of darkness on a disabled planet.

In this predicament, we search for a seer to guide us. We desire a visionary who can see through the shadows to find the light beyond. We need an explorer who is not bound by the existing maps and narratives of our possibilities. We need a man who can navigate the tenebrous turmoil of our times.

We need an explorer of human accomplishment who can tell us how to transcend a future that seems both dark and disabled. Providentially today, in this extraordinary manual of human triumph, we have the vision and wisdom that springs from the unique experiences of Redenbaugh. "Most people," he writes, "do not think about their lives until it is too late. Then they think only about their regrets." Despite his severe privations, Redenbaugh has lived a life of no regrets. This book gives us a lucid agenda for a radical shift in our own lives and in the future of our nation that will banish all regrets that stem from living too little and too lamely.

To Russell, the current human predicament is just life as he has known it from the age of 16. At that point, inspired by President Kennedy's declaration that by the end of the decade, America would put a man on the moon and bring him back alive, the young Redenbaugh attempted to build and launch a solid-state rocket out of an aluminum tube and some handmade gunpowder. The resulting explosion mangled his hands and caused him to lose his eyesight, first in one eye and then the other, despite a prolonged purgatory of some 30 surgeries. He was plunged into a life of darkness and disability. He was told he was destined to a regime of "welfare, unemployment, and dependency." His mother decided that he could never marry, attend a prestigious university, or even leave home.

It was the cautionary principle in practice. The world told Russell that he could not risk college, enterprise, marriage, or aspiration. He was condemned to the darkness of impotence and dependency.

This is our situation today as a nation. We incur debt to sustain ten million able young men without work and out of the workforce. We enact minimum wage laws that suppress the very starting jobs they need. We wrap the disabled in layers of programs and supports that end up making their disability insuperable.

Redenbaugh shows the path to redemption and prosperity not only intellectually but even physically and aspirationally. He became a national leader on the Civil Rights Commission, entrepreneurial creator in Silicon Valley, a partner in a prominent investment firm, husband and father, and even a world champion fully-abled athlete after age 50. I'll leave that remarkable triumph of age and guile over youth and strength for the book. It is an inspirational story for our particular times, dismissing the darkness of spurious psychology of human limits and asserting an agenda of supreme accomplishment.

Forced to shift, defy drift, compelled to pioneer in a suddenly darkened realm beyond most of our imaginations, he became an explorer of a mostly unknown sphere of human experience. He discovered that the chief obstacles to his success—and the success of other disabled people—come from the impulse to protect them from the world and the truth. In this book, he reveals his discoveries to the world, delivering a step-by-step agenda for shifts of thought, narrative, declaration, action, and perseverance that can radically change the lives of his readers and his country.

"Diversification is what you do when you don't know what to do," he writes. It means succumbing to the inexorably distracting diversity of the environment rather than moving forward in a coherent narrative toward your own goals. In response to the upholders of the existing rulebooks that prevail over our stagnant economy, our torpid lives, he quotes Cormac McCarthy: "If the rule you followed brought you to this, what use was the rule?"

We live in an economy of mind, and an economy of mind can change as quickly as minds can change. Redenbaugh changed his mind, and all else followed, as the apparent obstacles in his path gave way to opportunities, and the opportunities opened the way to new horizons. The key is knowing what you seek and saying it loud and publicly. "When the odds are against you," he writes, "and obstacles being thrown from many directions, having strong, clear declarations is what makes giving up on your narrative shift impossible. It closes the loopholes that allow you to slip-slide away from the design of your life."

Crucial is the willingness to flout drift and to shift the narrative of your life. Russell did it, and so can you. God punishes you chiefly for what you fail to imagine.

There is no easy way to change the world. As Redenbaugh reports, "My friend and student Leslie learned this while attending one of my investment seminars…She said that I taught her how to 'see' and found the irony of learning to see from a blind person absolutely delicious."

I learned much from this book and predict that many people will find the experience of learning to see from Redenbaugh's crisp prose and compelling stories similarly delectable.

—**George Gilder**, Tyringham, Massachusetts

INTRODUCTION

May 19, 1962

It must have been friction… or even just a spark.
Something ignited the fuel, and rather than just burning, it
exploded.

It must have been friction… or even just a spark.

Something ignited the fuel, and rather than just burning, it exploded.

The thunderous explosion could be heard several blocks away. On an otherwise lazy weekend morning, men, women, and children stopped what they were doing. They froze in place, with some even peering up anxiously at the sky, believing an enemy attack was never too far off.

Back in the middle of the charred, splintered garage, a teenage boy stood stunned in place with chest, arms, and face badly burned and gushing blood from shrapnel wounds.

I was surrounded by blackness, but there was no pain—yet.

I realized the rocket had exploded. I knew I was seriously injured…

DEFINITIONS USED IN THIS BOOK

1. NARRATIVE: Narratives are stories we tell ourselves. They are in part the way we make sense of the world in which we find ourselves. For example, "If I work hard and save money, I will prosper." Conversely, a negative narrative might be: "Nothing I do makes any difference; the game is rigged." These narratives have enormous power, as we shall see. Narratives can be true or false.

2. DECLARATIONS: Declarations are specific statements of intent such as "**I will not be poor**" or "**I will get an MBA from a prestigious University**." Declarations are Public, Specific, and Measurable.

3. DISTINCTIONS: A distinction separates things that may typically be grouped. For example, the distinction between what we want and what we will not tolerate. Distinctions include the definitions discussed below, assessments, assertions, promises, offers, and requests.

4. ASSESSMENTS: An assessment is an opinion. It can be grounded or ungrounded. Grounded means that there is

evidence to support the assessment. "Its cold today" is an assessment.

5. ASSERTIONS: An assertion is a statement of fact. "The thermometer reads 25 degrees Fahrenheit" is an Assertion. Twenty-five degrees might or might not be cold based on your location and season. For example, 25 degrees in Antarctica in winter would not be cold.

6. PROMISES: A promise is a contract between two or more people to perform a specific action by a time specified or assumed. For example, "I promise to be on time for dinner." Another example is "I do."

7. OFFERS: An offer is a conditional promise. For example, "I offer to cut your grass for $50". The offer is conditional on acceptance by the other party.

8. REQUESTS: A request is an act of asking for something. For example, "Please turn up the heat."

HOW TO SHIFT YOUR NARRATIVE

1. Identify what is causing your suffering, such as being poor

2. Declare what you will not tolerate, such as "I will not be poor."

3. Declare what you will do to move away from what you will not tolerate, such as "I will get an MBA from a prestigious university."

4. Take actions that are congruent with your goal, such as applying to a variety of MBA programs from prestigious universities until you are accepted

5. Have a way to measure your results, such as getting an MBA from a prestigious university or getting a high paying job

6. Periodically reevaluate

SHIFT

I want to share my journey with you not because I am special but because I am ordinary. Nevertheless, I changed my mind in a way that was not ordinary and have lived and am living an extraordinary life. I share this journey with you so you can learn the model and tools I developed by changing my narrative. I will help you shift the narrative of your life as I did mine.

When I was sixteen-years-old, I was injured, maimed, and blinded in a homemade rocket experiment gone wrong. From there, I had a choice to make—would I permit this new version of myself to define my life narrative moving forward? The answer was a firm no. Being blind would either limit or open my possibilities, and I chose the latter. After the accident, I shifted my narrative away from being a victim. I declared that being blind did not mean I would be needy, dependent, and homebound. I announced that I would not succumb to the narrative of what it is to be blind. I would live in the sighted world, doing things sighted people do. I lost my sight, but not my vision. Losing my sight compelled me to gain a vision for my future.

I went forward, a blind person in a sighted world, with sighted goals and a vision for my life not based on physical limitations. Determined to rise above welfare, I studied finance and investment, relentless in my pursuit of success. I refused to accept the denials that I heard from some of America's top universities' to mean that I should stop striving. The vision I had for my life was more open and less restricted than the one they saw for me. I had a more precise image than they did. I would become a partner in a billion-dollar investment firm. President Bush appointed me Commissioner on the U.S. Civil Rights Commission. I was the CEO of a software company in the early days of Silicon Valley. I founded my registered investment advisory firm. I acted as Chief Investment Officer for wealthy families and institutions. None of these things narrowed my focus. Instead, at age fifty, I took up the martial art of Brazilian Jiu-jitsu. I made an uncompromising commitment to training. I ended up becoming the sole blind black belt in the sport. I won three consecutive Brazilian Jiu-jitsu World Championships fighting sighted opponents. And I am not done achieving yet.

It saddens me how many of us don't believe we can write our own stories. As an economist, I think this is because people don't see the costs they're incurring by staying stuck. They are blind to the cost of not shifting their narrative. I'm sure that a psychologist, life coach, or another observer would give a very different answer—but I'm an economist. This is how I see and understand the world; in losses and gains, scarcity and abundance. In short, I see incentives. This view of the world, which I will show you in this book, is also the reason for Shift's title. I will show you here how to shift your life to a higher gear. We are not talking about a change in attitude or mood but a new way of motivating action. We are talking about becoming a different you. Traditionally life changes are fueled by motivation and inspiration, whether in book or speech form. Most of those messages last only until you close the book or return to your car after hearing the speech. Inspiration has its place. Yet, without effective action, it does not last, like last night's champagne. In sharp contrast, shifting your narrative is changing the story that may have supported you in the past but is now definitely holding you back.

While becoming blind was an accident, my journey from welfare to wealth was not. It was an intentional narrative shift, as were the other smaller navigations along the way. I'm about to share with you how I did it. You will not merely learn how I did what I have done. Far more importantly, you will see that you can do much more with your life than you ever thought possible. This book is about the journey *your* life can become by learning to see the world as I have learned to see it.

SECTION I
FLYING BLIND

The Myth of the Super Survivor

There is a literature of people who started as mere mortals and then, after surviving some enormous adversity, turned that adversity into a benefit and became very accomplished in one way or another. This is an effective way to think about your life. Because most people don't think about their life until it's too late. Then, they think only about their regrets.

—Russell Redenbaugh

CHAPTER 1
PURGATORY

During the early 1960s, Americans were very concerned about Communism. The Cold War, and what Ronald Reagan would call "The Evil Empire." The Soviet Union was ahead of us, particularly in weapons and space programs. They were first in space with the first satellite and early again with a human in orbit. Losing the Space Race wasn't OK with most of us, especially as they seemed related. The Space Race was not a friendly competition to reach the moon first. The race to the moon was a matter of national security.

President Kennedy declared that "We will put a man on the moon and bring him back alive in this decade." His declaration lit a fire under the country. There was a lot of nationalism mixed with concern that our enemies were taking over the world. That concern spread even to kids in high school, including me. The president's challenge was inspiring. I became enthusiastic about all things that flew.

One Saturday morning in Salt Lake City, where I was born, I anticipated summer break from the school I hated. I didn't have any work to do, so I decided to feed my passion for flight. It was a warm spring day, and I was working shirtless in our small garage. Outside in the sunlight, other kids played ball in the street. Women worked in their gardens, and men tinkered with Chevys and Fords in their driveways. In 1962, weekends weren't designed for anything more serious.

I was making a solid-state rocket. An aluminum tube served as the body. I made the fuel of sulfur, charcoal, and potassium nitrate. I designed the fuel to slow burn rather than explode like gunpowder. I'd obtained the sulfur from the local pharmacy. Regular grade barbeque charcoal was easy to come by. Getting my hands on potassium nitrate was a trickier affair. I pretended to be a delivery boy for Federated Milk Producers. I went to the Braun Connect and Hymen Chemical Supply Company to pick up "our" one-pound order. They bought my story, and I got the third ingredient for my homemade gunpowder.

My fingertips were growing black with gunpowder. Beads of sweat formed on the back of my neck in the warm, confined space. I was testing different mixtures of charcoal and sulfur. I needed to test to get the right burn rate. Sitting and sweating on a bench in a small work area in the garage, I got ready to clamp the rocket in a vise. A silver flash of light through the window blinded me as some neighborhood kids bicycled by. They were laughing and squealing, the bright spring sun reflecting off their bikes. I blinked hard to clear away the white spots and then returned to the task at hand, concentrating hard. After I clamped the rocket, the plan was to ignite it with an electric spark from my motorcycle's magneto. But I never got that far. While assembling it, something went wrong. **The rocket exploded**.

I felt the warm wet blood flowing over my skin, on my arms, my head, my chest, and my legs. Unable to see, I ran my hand down my leg and felt a heavy puddle of blood soaking through my jeans near my thigh. The bleeding was near a major artery I knew from Biology. If nobody came to my rescue soon, I would pass out and die. Thankfully, it took only seconds for most people from the neighborhood to arrive at the garage.

Our next-door neighbor, Ruth Johnson, was an Army surgical nurse. Luckily for me, it was 1962, and washer-dryers were not common. Ruth was gathering in her laundry that had been hanging out to dry. She rushed into the garage and used her sheets and blankets as bandages and tourniquets. I was floating in and out of consciousness, bleeding heavily, burned all over, and still unable to see.

I spent forty-two days in the hospital. My parents and my uncle Jake Garn visited every day. Jake was not yet a senator but had already been a fighter pilot and would later be in the space program. Every morning on his way to work, he came to relieve one of my parents, who slept in the room with me.

As the days and weeks passed in the hospital, I still had no idea how seriously injured I was. I knew I couldn't see, and I knew I couldn't feel my hands where the rocket had exploded. My parents and the doctors hid the extent of my injuries. Although well-meaning, they were misleading me.

"Well, you'll be able to do anything you could have done before," Mother lied, trying to protect me from the grim truth.

The reality of my medical situation was that I had needed eight pints of blood to survive. I'd lost one eye immediately in the explosion but still had partial vision in my remaining eye. Then there were my hands, still a mystery, hidden deep in layers of red-stained gauze bandages.

During one of many surgeries, the doctors decided to keep me awake but sedated with painkillers. They wanted to see how much mobility and feeling I had in my (remaining) fingers. I was aware, and I could see, not well, but well enough. As the doctors probed, prodded, and tested, I lifted my head a few inches off the pillow and peered down at my hands. Through the snow-white drugged haze, I saw the mangled mess of my hands. I couldn't tell the difference between fingers and knuckles. I couldn't tell where my hands ended and wrists began. I dropped my head back onto the pillow, sure that I had hallucinated the whole horrifying sight. Unfortunately, I had not.

DETACHED

After six weeks in the hospital and a few dozen surgeries, it was time for me to return to life, my new normal. Even with one eye lost in the accident, my eyesight was good enough to drive a car for short distances only but well enough to be safe. There was one lingering caveat. Some of the shrapnel from the explosion that almost killed me lodged behind the retina. The shrapnel threatened my remaining eye. Here is where I entered purgatory, living in limbo between what was and what might be, but it was not yet clear.

The doctors told me to avoid most physical activities. This restriction supposedly reduced the risk of the fragile retina detaching. The surgical team restricted me to home, except for surgeries. I navigated the world with eyes that saw differently and hands that felt different. It was the condition of my hands that upset me the most. I thought, "It would have been better if I was blind with my hands intact." Be careful about wishes.

Purgatory (n): a place of temporary suffering or misery

Purgatory is a frustrating place to live. I don't recommend it at all if you can avoid it. My peers, now seniors in high school, enjoyed the gift of planning their futures. Some prepared for Mormon Missions. Some prepped for college. I could not prepare for anything because nobody knew how the eye surgeries would turn out. I was at the mercy of my situation with no choices. Unable to move much, my mind took flight, moving back and forth between hope and fear.

"I'm not the person I was, but I don't know whom I'm going to be. Who will want me? Who will date me? Who will value me? Who will hire me?"

Most people never realize they're living in purgatory because it has seemed normal for so long. Because my version of purgatory was so pronounced and different, I was fully aware of it. I wanted to crawl out of my skin the whole time.

My last surgery was nine months after the rocket exploded in my hands and took out one of my eyes. I lay in the hospital bed after the surgery with the "good" eye in postoperative bandages. Mother perched anxiously on the edge of the bedside chair. We were about to receive the verdict on my eyesight and my life moving forward. Father stayed back home in Salt Lake, running our family-owned candy factory. He also worked a part-time job to pay my medical bills.

I heard two doctors walk into the room. I could sense their reluctance because they didn't come bustling in as usual. Usually, after surgeries, there were daily business sounds and voice tones. This time was different. They walked with hesitant steps. Neither Doctor wanted to have this conversation with me. And then…

"We have done all we can do. He will be blind for the rest of his life," one of the doctors said, speaking in slow, halting tones.

The other doctor stood beside him. He fiddled nervously with his stethoscope, as I could hear, not saying a word.

I felt incredible relief after months of unbearable tension and uncertainty! Already completely blind in one eye from the explosion, I wondered about the other for so long. With the verdict, the purgatory walls came crashing to the ground, and I finally felt *free*! Free to plan, to explore options, to take action, to move forward.

The surgeons grabbed a box of tissues, handed it to my hysterical mother, and rushed out of the room. Surgeons didn't have the best bedside manner. These two couldn't wait to get back into surgical scrubs and grab their scalpels.

The narrative they projected for me was bleak and powerless. Blind people in 1963 had few options. Common options were to remain uneducated, work in a sheltered workshop or sell pencils on the street corner, which is a form of begging. I would get a guide dog, a collapsible stick, and the limiting label "handicapped." I rejected not only this label but also the entire narrative built around it.

How did I make such a bold decision, young and traumatized as I was? My father was instrumental. He read me inspirational books and poems at my bedside.

I am often guided by the same quote from William Ernest Henley's poem *Invictus* that my father read aloud. This quote helped push me to action from my hospital bed.

> Out of the night that covers me,
>   Black as the pit from pole to pole,
> I thank whatever gods may be
>   For my unconquerable soul.
>
> In the fell clutch of circumstance
>   I have not winced nor cried aloud.
> Under the bludgeonings of chance
>   My head is bloody, but unbowed.
>
> Beyond this place of wrath and tears
>   Looms but the Horror of the shade,

And yet the menace of the years
    Finds and shall find me unafraid.

It matters not how strait the gate,
    How charged with punishments the scroll,
I am the master of my fate,
    I am the captain of my soul.

Left with my unglued, sobbing mother, I knew it was up to me to take action. It had been less than an hour since the Doctors told me I would be entirely blind for life.

Mother was a legal secretary. I thought that if I could occupy her mind with a familiar task, it might bring her back from the abyss.

"Mother, I want you to take a letter," I said.

She became silent for a moment. Then, by force of habit, she grabbed a notepad and wrote down what I said. This single task got her mind off the bleak future. She was back in the present and taking action.

The letter was to Guide Dogs for the Blind in San Rafael, California. Years later, I realized that I was making a declaration that would shape my life's story by taking this action.

President Kennedy had made his space declaration two years earlier. So as a teenage boy in his garage in Salt Lake City, I fell in love with flight. I became enamored with the Space Race, but unfortunately, I was no rocket scientist.

Lying in that hospital bed, I vowed to take action to change the course of my life. The president's passion for freeing oneself from limitations inspired me to find a way to fly. In my case, I would be flying blind. I vowed not to let it stop me from living a life that I defined—not one decided by others.

CHAPTER 2
ROBBING BANKS

W e live in a world where all too often, people pop a pill to quell nerves or depressing thoughts. They medicate to suppress mental or physical pain. People often overlook the power of taking action. Action always produces a better mood. It is inaction and inactivity that are painful.

While I waited for the verdict on my eyesight, the pain of boredom and purgatory was enforced inaction, for example. I could have asked for some sort of prescription-grade remedy. Instead, I endured the daily battle of wanting to crawl out of my skin. The doctor's final verdict was, "there's nothing else we can do for you. You will be blind for the rest of your life" I found it ironic that only then did Mother and the doctors think I should see a psychiatrist to "process." I felt nothing but relief at the opportunity to leave purgatory and finally get on with my life. I thought they were the crazy ones for suggesting such a thing. My prognosis relieved the torture of inactivity, the anxiety of uncertainty, and the depression of boredom.

With Mother's grief at bay, I could focus on my declarations for the future. In the San Francisco Children's Hospital, where I was sent for eye surgery in 1963, I didn't call these thoughts and actions I was having "declarations." And I certainly did not know these declarations were a crucial tool to shift my narrative. I did see that I was identifying what I wouldn't tolerate about my life. Making this shift closed some possibilities while opening the door for others. The actions I would take would support the opportunities that remained.

Since the Doctors could do no more for me, Mother and I headed back home to Salt Lake City. Besides my eyesight and hands, I was a healthy teenage boy who still had one year of high school to complete.

Word had spread quickly about my prognosis. When our plane touched down, most of the family had gathered at the airport, waiting to see me. There was Father, my brother, and aunts and uncles, including Uncle Jake.

Mother and I emerged from the flight ramp into the airport. I found it odd that an airline employee was pushing me in a wheelchair since there was nothing at all wrong with my legs. Back then, as now, that's how people treat the blind. People think blind or handicapped are synonymous with helpless. How wrong they were.

I was more self-conscious about my mostly missing left hand than my blindness. In California, we purchased a cosmetic prosthesis that slid on like a glove over what remained of my hand. It looked like a full left hand. I arranged my hands in my lap in a resting position, with the plastic left one stacked over the real right one. This position also concealed the missing thumb and index finger on my right hand. Even though Uncle Vern knew the condition of my hands, he seemed impressed with the display. I think he was also comforted, protected from the jarring sight of my actual hands. The illusion was more comfortable for everyone.

"Oh, he has a nice way of holding his hands now," Uncle Vern commented.

He didn't realize I was wearing the prosthesis but could tell something was different. His reaction amused me. I only ended up wearing the thing for a year before deciding it was unnecessary.

It was early spring, and guide dog school wouldn't come until after summer. It was back to high school for me a few days after getting home. Once again, I was relieved and almost jubilant to have purposeful actions—go back to school, attend class, study, take exams, and finish high school. I was also thrilled to be someplace other than in a hospital with Mother after the five eye surgeries in San Francisco.

My classmates had only gotten a brief glimpse of me in August with my prosthetic eye. My remaining eye, which still had some vision, was obscured behind thick coke bottle glasses so heavy that they had to be hooked behind my ears to stay up. "Some vision" was very generous since my vision was 20/400 with 20/200 being legally blind.

I was in medical seclusion from September until February to protect my good eye from further injury. I was a different person now, about to reenter the seeing world. My declaration that I would not be poor, unmarriageable, homebound, helpless, or "handicapped" would soon be put to the test.

One thing happened right away that added fuel to my declaration. I didn't have a guide dog yet, and I was in no way proficient in cane travel. I found myself feeling my way along walls, lockers, and around doorways. I clumsily tapped my cane on any obstacle in my path, trying to figure out what it was. If the object moved and turned out to be a living being, I had to remember to stop hitting it. That kind of thing wouldn't make me popular with my classmates. Navigating this way, trying not to fall over and end up sprawled on a hallway floor as roadkill, was difficult enough with no one around. But when the bell rang, the hallways became roaring oceans of teenagers, 2700 of them. Swarms of sighted students flowed like a fast-moving riptide in every possible direction. I was afraid I'd get swept up and unceremoniously spit out into the parking lot. The academic powers-that-be permitted me to leave my classes five minutes early. This gave me time to get to my next destination before the hallways filled with rowdy students. I didn't want to resort to walking around on the elbow of an escort. That went against my declaration to not be dependent on others.

Something happened that fueled my declaration further. I was hugging the wall, tapping awkwardly away, en route to my next class. I walked by two janitors who thought I couldn't hear them. Perhaps blind and deaf went hand in hand to them.

"Isn't that the most pitiful thing you've ever seen?" one janitor said to the other. "It might have been better for him and everyone else if he had died," responded the other.

I don't think they were intentionally unkind. The janitor's words simply reflected the attitude of people at the time. Their comments reflected an unexamined narrative. I understood that. But I still took it to heart, and it added fuel to my fire of personal independence. I saw I wasn't alone in this distinction. Many people saw me as out of the game.

This thinking isn't limited to the disabled: You're the wrong color. You're in the wrong club. You're not playing our game. You're out of it.

Even my friends were affected by this narrative. Since the accident, things got awkward, and they divided themselves into two groups: the few who moved closer and the majority who drifted away. Growing up in Salt Lake City at that time, most of us were, of course, Mormons. We were racing toward graduation day, and people were making their plans. Most were going to college. The most significant percentage defaulted to the local University of Utah. A small number were heading to out-of-state schools. Some were fellow Mormons going on a mission for the LDS church.

At that time, church members assumed male Mormons would go on a thirty-month mission, often to a foreign country. The flock or family would support these uncompensated missions. Missionaries lived in humble conditions. One friend who was on that path assumed that I would be disappointed about not going. Honestly, I had not been called to go on a mission. I had enough trouble tapping around the school hallways. Forget trying to navigate my way around a foreign country. I had no regrets whatsoever.

My plan was and had always been to go to college. I knew that having no education or skills would condemn me to welfare, unemployment, and dependency. I decided that lack of skills would make me a disabled citizen, not my lack of physical eyesight. My mother had a different opinion. Like most people, she "knew" that I would never be able to leave home and never be able to marry.

I still wasn't thinking of these beliefs that were forming as "declarations fueled by action that are the tools needed to shape my life narrative." I was just thinking of what I needed to do and what I needed not to do.

I was also thinking about proving wrong the people who saw me from their preconceived "disabled" attitudes.

WHERE THE MONEY IS

Once I had my high school diploma, the next step was college. The University of Utah had to accept all in-state students, so the next stage of my education was easy. It was a low-cost university to begin with, plus I was on welfare, which paid for the education. **Education may be the only smart use for welfare.** The other types of benefits make you promise to stay in purgatory no matter what. Do not work, do not save, do not invest, and do not marry the father of your children. Any single one of these promises is likely to destroy a life, and all four clearly will.

A declaration always opens and closes possibilities. If your declaration, like mine, is to be independent, then wasting time at the beach all year is inconsistent and therefore ruled out. Using welfare money to stay unemployed, stay home, and stay stupid, are ruled out as well. Once we rule out enough possibilities, we arrive at actions consistent with the declaration. Get into the University of Utah. Live at home to reduce costs. Get a degree. Acquire skills that will be valued. The last one helped me choose a major. Many students go about choosing a major from all the possibilities. I went in reverse, using a process of elimination. By stating, "**Get skills that will be valued**," I immediately ruled out dozens of majors. I didn't major in underwater basket-weaving, for instance. My declaration had me rule out the "no job degrees" in favor of the "job degrees." I chose banking, finance, accounting, and most of all, economics. As the notorious bank robber, Willie Sutton said when asked why he robbed banks, "Because that's where the money is." So I studied banking and finance because that's where the money is.

By making these decisions, I also solved some of the social challenges of college, like popularity. Remember that I was a mediocre student in high school at best, never the Brainiac of any group. Now, at the University of Utah, in a serious major and powered by the declaration to get new skills and a good job (plus a date), I became a valuable social commodity to some of the other students. As a freshman, I was quickly recruited into a fraternity so my frat brothers could continue to party. At the same time, my 4.0 GPA brought up the house average, thereby keeping the party going. Rather than feeling used, I enjoyed this turn of events as a good student. It was like going from being the kid picked last at baseball to the one picked first. I didn't do the things bad students do because it didn't fit my new narrative. My declaration's strength and focus on succeeding no matter what transformed me from a low-performing high school student to graduating first in my class.

This new path, college into an investment career, required a complete change of my previous life narrative. I no longer assumed I would just drift into the family business and take over. Thus, I rewrote the narrative of my life. When I realized I would be blind forever, I realized that I would not be taking over the family's candy manufacturing business. I knew I needed to prepare myself for a different life than I had assumed.

CHAPTER 3
OUT OF THE DARKNESS

Within an hour of finding out that I would never see again, I took action. I dictated a letter to my mother to apply for admission to a guide dog school in San Rafael. If blindness kept me from the independent, prosperous life I desired, I would need a companion who could guide me. I started putting my declaration, to never be dependent on others, into action. That summer after high school graduation, my friends celebrated. Then they prepared for college or their Mormon missions. I went back to school to meet my new best friend of the four-legged variety.

The guide dog school was free, supported by contributions and endowments. Founded after World War II by the U.S. Army canine corps office, the school trained dogs for blind veterans. The school

17

buildings were World War II-era temporary wooden structures. It sat on fifteen or twenty acres.

The curriculum ran for twenty-eight days, but it was three or four days before we even got our dogs. We did much sitting and waiting. That's when students got to know one another. There were fifteen students, divided into two basic categories: those born blind and those who had once been able to see. A lot of the blind population in the early 1960s were incubator babies whose eyes had been damaged by excessive oxygen as preemies. The other group was older people who were blind from age-related optical issues. I was the only one who had lost eyesight from trauma. I tended to hang out with the people who had once been able to see as we had more in common.

My anticipation of getting the dog assigned to me built. I felt like I was in limbo again, desperately wanting to take action. Bring on the next step in the journey of my life!

My family had a dog growing up. While I understand that all living creatures are remarkable, our dog in Salt Lake City was unremarkable. It was untrained and had few requirements beyond feeding, walking, and cleaning up after it. I was curious to find out how a trained "professional" dog would be different.

They trained us on the basics of guide dog care. Then they tested our stamina, walking speed, and mobility. I got more and more impatient with all the pre-training. I wondered what breed of dog I would get, the name, and the gender. I was like a kid counting down the days until Christmas! Finally, they brought me the key to my mobility. Her name was Minka, and she was a sixty-five-pound female German shepherd.

The guide dogs were already ninety percent trained which is a very high standard. We spent the first day getting to know our dogs. I made a pact with Minka to figure out this whole new partnership together, and we shook on it.

Minka was a funny one. She thought that if she couldn't see other people, they couldn't see her. She would hide her head behind a telephone pole, the way an ostrich puts his head in the ground. Minka didn't understand "blind." She learned as part of the training; if she didn't move, I would step on her. Once we became acquainted, it was time to go on our very first walk together. It was morning, the sun had come up, and I could smell the dew. I finally had my legs back and was ready for my newfound freedom. The moment that Minka and I took our first steps together, I felt reborn. It was like the line from *Oliver*, "I now know how it feels to fly through the streets with wings on my heels." It was the first time since losing my eyesight that I could walk at a rapid pace without fear of falling. It was the first time I could walk without "guidance" from a sighted person who had no idea how to lead a blind person. I was a free man again!

We learned in guide school to always follow your dog. If you disobey your dog, you may fall into a trench. They know what you're doing, and you do not. I thought I'd listened.

Minka and I practiced all over San Rafael and then San Francisco. Navigating sidewalks, crosswalks, local stores, elevators, escalators, bus rides, and busy city environments. I obediently let Minka take the lead, and she never led me wrong. When we got back home to Salt Lake City, my ego took charge, and I walked very quickly around the streets where I'd grown up. Suddenly Minka came to an abrupt stop and would not budge. I urged her forward, corrected her, and finally got her to step ahead. Whack! I ran right into the low branch of a tree. She was doing her job, but I wasn't doing mine! Minka and I would continue to have our adventures together over the years. My relationship with a guide dog opened a whole new world based on one single declaration of independence. And I was determined to learn to navigate that world.

CHAPTER 4
REJECTION

If the rule you followed brought you to this,
of what use was the rule?
—**Cormac McCarthy**, No Country for Old Men

1967

y hospital bed **declarations** were:

I will not be poor.
I will not be dependent on others.
I will not live at home, be led to the bathroom, fed, and walked.
I will live an active, independent life and be valued by sighted people.

All of these would require getting a job.

I'd graduated first in my class from the University of Utah. In other words, I had a diploma from an undistinguished university in the Western mountains. I realized this wouldn't be good enough for the successful career I envisioned. My job prospects weren't excellent. I needed more skills and credentials and knew that the "hot degree" at the time was an MBA.

My next declaration was: **I will get an MBA from a prestigious university.**

As with any declaration, it needed to be immediately accompanied by action. MBAs don't fall out of the sky. I applied to Harvard and Stanford. Stanford accepted and processed my application and my $25 check. Then they let me know that a blind person would not be able to graduate from their school. Twenty-five dollars might not seem like much money now. Twenty-five dollars was one hundred gallons of gasoline at the time, a lot for a student on welfare. Being better endowed, Harvard sent the check back when they came to the same conclusion.

How could either school know that a blind person couldn't graduate from their MBA program if neither had admitted anyone blind? Their declarations lacked logic, but they had the authority to decide if I could attend or not.

I will get an MBA from a prestigious university.

I rallied my friends, family, and other contacts and organized a letter-writing campaign to Stanford. I thought my chances were better there, and I hoped they would admit me. The campaign resulted in an outpouring of support from professors and students. One student even crafted a well-articulated challenge letter to the Stanford powers-that-be. He stated, "I have to wonder why Stanford feels it isn't up to the challenge of educating someone who is blind." The pressure continued. One of Stanford's alumni donors, the eponymous O.C. Tanner, founder of the well-known Utah jewelry company, stood up for me. Stanford did end up reconsidering my application, and this time reached a different conclusion.

"We are now convinced that we were wrong, that you could graduate from our program. But it's our responsibility not to waste one of our slots on someone who is obviously unemployable," they wrote.

Even with my modest education and lack of eyesight, there was one thing I knew for sure about myself—I was much more than a wasted slot.

Keep in mind that this unfolded before the Higher Education Act of 1965, which legally prevented such discrimination. It was a time when things were much more transparent and authentic than they are now. At that time, there was less political correctness, and people spoke their minds. Stanford and Harvard wouldn't be able to refuse me today. Is this progress? As much as the rejections stung at the time, I don't think so. Both schools declared their honest assessment of my chances at success in their programs no matter their biases. I wish I had had this sage and level-headed perspective back then.

The resounding "nos" were a significant setback from my declaration, but I needed to take the next action and keep moving forward.

I will get an MBA from a prestigious university.

Next, I asked, which is the number three school? It was the University of Pennsylvania's Wharton School of Business. I also had a number four school lined up and would find number five, six, and so on if that's what it took to make good on my declaration. As the saying goes, "When Plan A doesn't work out, keep going because there are twenty-five other letters in the alphabet." I never thought, "Oh well, got rejected, might as well go work in the family business." That action would be inconsistent with the declaration that **I will get an MBA from a prestigious university**. When the odds are against you, and there are many obstacles, you need something special. That something is having healthy, explicit declarations. That is what makes giving up on your narrative shift impossible.

My declaration was not specifically to get an MBA from Harvard or Stanford, so Wharton met the requirement. There is a lesson here when you're writing your declarations. Make the wording specific enough to prompt explicit, focused action. Do not make your declaration so narrow that it closes too many possibilities and makes failure inevitable. There is only one Harvard, so if my declaration was, "I will get an MBA from Harvard," that would have ruled out other valid schools. It also makes Harvard the endpoint rather than a path to something else. The MBA and finance were the paths, not the destination. I took the long train ride from Salt Lake City to Philadelphia to meet with Wharton's Dean of Admissions, Dr. Blanchard. I went there to allow him to make Harvard and Stanford look bad. His declaration started the same as the others, but then it veered in a different direction.

"Well, I don't know if you can make it here or not because we've never admitted a person who is blind to our school," he said.

"But you're admitted anyway. I'm not even going to take this to the committee. You're admitted, and if you can't make it here, you'll have to leave, like anyone else who can't do the work. You will have the same chance as any other student."

What a difference between Stanford and Harvard his words were. We shook hands. It took persistence, but I found the opportunity that aligned with my declaration. I found an option that benefitted both parties. Look for these kinds of opportunities once you write your declarations.

Years later, I would found an investment company called Kairos Capital Advisors. Kairos is Greek, meaning, "That moment when vision, bold action, and opportunity converge to achieve extraordinary accomplishment."

IN THE GAME

Now that I was acquiring skills, my next declaration was: **I will get a job in the investment business.**

Once again, I put myself near the top of my class, this time in the number five spot. Mother wanted to know what the other four did that I did not. Behind every successful man, there is an unsatisfiable mother.

As graduation neared and job offers showered my classmates, Stanford's assessment started appearing correct. I could not get a job. Meanwhile, my peers would have four or five interviews and get three offers. Some got offers even without the interview, usually from second-tier consulting or banking firms. Many received large signing bonuses. I couldn't even get a bite from the federal government. I had forty-nine job interviews and not a single offer.

Fear grabbed hold of me. Just the word "unemployed" created images of welfare, homelessness, and moving back home to live with my parents. The mere thought haunted me at night. Unemployment was an unacceptable narrative with no connection to my declarations. I would keep looking for a job until I got one. That was the only possibility.

I will get a job in the investment business.

Then, a serendipitous connection turned things around. My classmate Robert Arthur received an offer from Cooke & Bieler, a tiny investment-counseling firm in Philadelphia.

Robert was hoping to bring me along with him to Cooke & Bieler. The problem was that it was a six-professional firm, and that year they'd already hired their quota of two new MBAs. They didn't want a third one. But because of Robert's high praise for me, they agreed to an interview. I met with one of the partners, Jim McLennan. Much to my surprise, they made me an offer! It was a conditional offer like Wharton's, "We don't know if this will work, but we're willing to try, and if it doesn't, you'll have to leave." That was more than good enough for me. I had a job in the investment business.

I had many responsibilities at Cooke & Bieler in the beginning. Responsibilities included research-based security analyses of companies and their stocks. Writing reports, making presentations, and managing client portfolios took up most of my time. The team did travel research, visited companies at their headquarters, and interviewed management. We analyzed financials and industry and reached conclusions about what to buy and up to what price. It was all entry-level work. I dug in with a ferocious work ethic, learning as much as possible and determined to have great success in this profession.

The conditional offer that got me in the door at Cooke & Bieler would be utterly illegal after The Americans with Disabilities Act passed in 1990. They would not have been allowed to employ me under the condition of hiring my own sighted assistant. The firm would have been guilty of discrimination since they didn't make "reasonable accommodation" as that law requires. A "reasonable accommodation" might include changes to the workplace to navigate "safely and without harm." They might have had to change office equipment for me to use it or provide a reader to help me do my work. "Reasonable accommodation" is one reason, in my opinion, that the unemployment rate for the seriously disabled has not changed. It may have increased since the ADA became law. It stops companies from doing what Cooke & Bieler did, offer someone a chance, which puts the employer in jeopardy. The jeopardy comes not from trying to skirt special accommodations rules (which Cooke & Bieler never attempted to do), but because no business wants to take a chance on an employee that they cannot terminate if necessary. It is simply not a smart business practice. If you find the above confusing, it is not your fault; the law is confusing.

Employers are put at risk whenever they hire a member of any "protected class." The only thing that members of the class are protected from is being employed! Cooke & Bieler would have said (amongst each other in private, of course), "Are you crazy? We already hired two MBAs, and you want us to hire a third who's fireproof?" But without it, I got the job.

CONGRESSIONAL COMPASS

By the early 1970s, I was a partner at Cooke & Bieler, having worked my way up from analyst to portfolio manager to Chief Investment Officer. During my time there, I had the honor of being mentored in finance by one of the greatest economic thinkers, Art Laffer, creator of the "Laffer Curve." Art's story began in the mid-1970s when the world was in a state of economic confusion and turmoil. In 1974, Art dined in Washington D.C. with Dick Cheney, Donald Rumsfeld, and political economist Jude Wanniski. By the main course, Art found himself unsuccessfully trying to explain a new economic concept he'd been working on that he called the Laffer Curve. He grabbed one of the linen napkins from the upscale restaurant table, asked the waiter for a Sharpie marker, and drew a picture of the curve.

I became a fan of the Laffer Curve and brought the supply-side economics story through Cooke & Bieler's front doors by bringing Art on as an advisor. Some of my associates were skeptical at such a wild economic theory, but I stood firm. One of the first things I did was take Art out to lunch at a local Japanese sushi restaurant on the same block as the firm. Once there, I shamelessly asked him to recreate the "dinner napkin." Art obliged. He found a linen napkin and drew his diagram, describing to me what he was sketching. I have that napkin today, framed on a wall in my house.

One axis of the inverted U shaped curve represents tax rates, and the other, tax revenues. The curve shows that two tax rates will produce the same revenues: the zero tax rate will have zero revenues, and the hundred percent tax rate will also have zero revenues. Many believed that this idea of tax rates and lowering tax rates could increase revenue was pretty wacky. But it caught on, and history has proven its merit. In parallel, it's also why stores that have sales often increase their profits. Lower prices can result in higher profits.

The Laffer Curve became a significant influencer of government economic policy. I had a front-row seat observing the intersection of policy and investing. This new narrative of how government policies direct economies and set global asset prices became a powerful one in my life.

Understanding the power of policy, particularly monetary and tax policy, I wanted an appointment to the Federal Reserve Board. The Board sets monetary policy. I admit that this opportunity only existed in the first place because Uncle Jake was a U.S. Senator and also chair of the Senate Banking Committee. Jake went to the Senate Majority Leader at the time, Bob Dole, to see about an appointment for me. Senator Dole had just appointed another person and didn't want to push his privilege such a short time later. I was disappointed, but Senator Dole came back with a different idea of how I could get into the government influence game.

"What I do want you to do, and I would consider it a personal favor, is to be on the U.S. Civil Rights Commission. I have the power of appointment this year. I want to appoint someone who is disabled but doesn't make a living from being disabled," said Senator Dole, in his matter-of-fact Midwestern way.

Bob Dole was disabled. In World War II, he was in the 10th Mountain Division, a ski-based fighting unit in the Italian Alps. He took a bullet in his right hand and arm and was disabled as a result. He was unable to use his right hand and arm, such that he had to shake left-handed.

There was only one way for me to respond.

"Senator Dole, I am honored, and I accept."

It was a part-time job, and I didn't have to leave my investment partnership in Philadelphia. I would serve about forty hours a month on the commission, taking a short train ride down to the Capitol for a day or two each month. We also had investigative field trips and the power to subpoena documents and witnesses. I was now in Washington about to begin affecting policy.

I quickly learned the harsh realities of causing real change in Washington. Like many things in our government, the Civil Rights Commission doesn't accomplish much. This is by design. There are eight commissioners, the perfect number for a maddening record of ties and deadlocked decisions. It's a poor design, and I fully credit the government for having planned it.

In 1958 the commission was created by the Eisenhower administration. It descended into politics, with the Left sometimes controlling the game and the Right at other times. The ball would get passed from one side to the other, and the game would continue with no real winner or progress made.

One of the more productive things that came from serving on the commission was that I learned how to write dissents. Dissents are the Civil Rights Commission's official opinions on various national situations, for instance, the presidential election of 2000.

The commission gave me the job, with Abby Thernstrom, to write the dissent in the Bush V. Gore election. Some believed that Bush stole the election. We wrote a fifty-four-page dissent, which was unusually long, but the situation was unusual. Our report addressed a specific allegation about Catherine Harris, the Republican Secretary of State of Florida. The story was that she conspired with twenty different county commissioners, including Democrats, to rig Florida's presidential vote. There was no evidence to support this claim. I brought up how difficult it was to get volunteers to become good at anything they do only once every four years. If the allegations were true, this was indeed a masterful scheme by knowledgeable and skilled individuals. I'm not sure if that kind of personal wit made it into the report since the final drafts were more courtroom-style than cable news commentary. We hired some experts on voting statistics. They produced a decisive statistical refutation to support our position.

The final dissent expanded to seventy-one pages. We used statistical methods to show the election was fair. Voting patterns were consistent with previous elections. There wasn't any improper influence by Catherine Harris. She would not have been able to influence Democratic country commissioners. There was a lot of testimony stating otherwise, but testimony is not evidence. Consistent with my viewpoint of the world as an economist, we used evidence.

My next chapter on the Civil Rights Commission came when we identified some funny stuff going on with money. It was not funny, but rather criminal, missing money and money spent on unnecessary travel and expenses. A commissioner and a staffer were having both an affair and a money arrangement. At the time, there was a divided government. The Republican, Bush 43, was hamstrung by a Democrat congress.

Those of us in the minority on the commission demanded an audit to determine what happened to the money. I led a group to reorganize the entire commission. We wanted to clean up all the abuses after it became clear that divided government would soon end. It was clear that Republicans would make the next appointment, and Republicans would finally have the majority and be free to make meaningful changes. I wanted Democrats and Republicans to agree on these changes. I'd learned in business by then that agreements are more successful and permanent than when one side bullies the other.

Let's be clear that this wasn't a political problem I was trying to fix, but an organizational design problem. It was a redesign of the organization to make it more transparent, authentic, and useful. As expected, I got a lot of pushback from the Democrats. But to my surprise, I received an equal amount of objection from the incoming Republicans. I realized what was happening was even more criminal than I thought.

Some of the Republicans' thinking on the commission seemed to be, "You don't understand. It's going to be our turn soon, and then we wield political power. But if your reforms are adopted, Russell, none of it will be allowed." This political gamesmanship became clear to me as I testified before the Committee of Congress about our group's flaws. I recommended that Congress suspend, defund, and end the Civil Rights Commission. I told them they had the power to kill the commission, and that's what they should do.

Killing the commission wasn't an impossible idea. President Reagan closed several agencies with bipartisan support (not as many as he promised he would, but he did cut entire agencies). In this case, they couldn't get that bipartisan agreement. Neither party wanted to take responsibility for the headline "they killed the Civil Rights Commission." Both sides rejected the challenge I laid down for them as too big of a risk. I made a new declaration that serving on the commission wasn't something I was willing to tolerate under these circumstances, so I quit. I couldn't see how to stay. I wasn't resentful or punitive. There was no blaming of specific individuals. I was stating the facts. "This is not working. Here are the things you need to do. Either close it or do these things; either way, I'm gone." As a side note, it occurs to me that since I was on the commission for fifteen years, either they or I were very slow learners.

If you'd like to read the media coverage of my resignation, I'd suggest you search on the Internet, "Russell Redenbaugh quits Civil Rights Commission." Hopefully, my opinions will provide some insights into our government policymakers' inner workings. These policy shenanigans don't only happen in the Civil Rights Commissions. They occur in dealings that affect the growth of our twenty trillion dollar economy. These corrupt policies jeopardize the prosperity of our 330 million citizens. As the New York Times wrote in 2005, "*Russell G. Redenbaugh, who served on the United States Commission on Civil Rights for 15 years, has resigned, saying that the agency had become too partisan and that "chronic mismanagement" had caused severe financial problems. "The commission, once the nation's conscience, is now a national embarrassment beyond repair," Mr. Redenbaugh said in his resignation letter, adding that he was frustrated with his colleagues' resistance to an independent review."*

I left Washington aware of the power of policy and what it meant for investors. This policy-based investing narrative is not one Wall Street likes. It is a narrative that I would rely on many times over my investing career.

My civil rights experience also demonstrates the importance of making decisions based on your own North Star. Have you ever been put in a position that you knew went against your beliefs and declarations? How did that feel? You likely felt a sense of discomfort, which came from your ideas being out of alignment with your circumstances, which is called "cognitive dissonance." Avoiding cognitive dissonance is one reason why declarations are essential. If you haven't established what you will and will not accept, how will you identify situations where you must decide? I was put in a position where I had to decide. Not only did I resign, but I did it live on CSPAN.

THE BIGGEST SHIFT

By the mid-1980s, the Soviet Union was on the brink of collapse. I saw strong possibilities on the horizon for the United States, especially from an investment standpoint. At Cooke & Bieler, we ran the business appropriately as long as the "evil empire" stood and the Cold War quietly raged. Then, when the Soviet Union disappeared almost overnight, there was talk of a "peace dividend." My partners argued that the dividend wouldn't be that great because military spending could not drop very much. The future risk to present assets would be so much less without the Soviet threat. They were thinking like accountants, and they were right in terms of accounting. I argued that the peace dividend had much larger implications. Beyond lower spending, the peace dividend also meant there was no longer a threat of nuclear annihilation. The removal of that threat, I predicted, had a high value in financial markets. It would be a positive factor for income, output, employment, and stock prices for decades.

I found myself at odds with my partners at Cooke & Bieler around the very issue I had been learning since my hospital bed, narratives matter. Investors live in narratives about the present and the future, which they expect to be better or worse. These narratives can dramatically alter asset valuations and affect market prices. The end of the Cold War produced a boom in the general economy and technology specifically. The story my partners were missing, but I was seeing, was that the end of the Soviet Union would unleash freedom, opportunity, and prosperity around the globe. I believed the stock market would notice. I ended up being correct; in response to better economic policies, US stocks advanced fifteen times in the 1980s and 1990s. Having the right narrative can make you a lot of money. The narrative disagreement caused me to turn my sights to opportunities beyond Cooke & Bieler.

As the Soviet Union was falling, Silicon Valley was rising. I had been spending more and more time in California analyzing technology companies for Cooke & Bieler. I'd also become a student of Dr. Fernando Flores, who owned a software company dedicated to making corporations more efficient. He designed an email-based project management application for businesses. He designed it to improve action, project coordination, and project completion.

The more time I spent immersed in the West Coast's future, the more uninspiring it became to go back East to the ongoing investment narrative conflict. I felt like a racehorse in a traffic jam.

My partners at Cooke & Bieler continued to make incorrect assessments about the new world following the fall of the Berlin Wall.

At the same time, Dr. Flores was surfing the information superhighway. He was anticipating the enormous disruptive force of the internet. He was cracking codes to revolutionize corporate America. The speed of the change of digital technology beckoned me. I knew where I wanted to be.

Thus, it was time for a new narrative and a new declaration to set me on the path toward it. **I will become a technology investor/consultant.**

Next was the matter of taking actions that supported my new declaration. I needed a job in technology. Studying philosophy and neurobiology with Dr. Flores and helping him with his business, I told him that I was available for another career opportunity if he knew of anything. He promptly made me an offer to be CEO of his software company.

This decision had significant risks. I was walking away from a shockingly high income, I had no idea if I was doing the right thing, and the software industry was very new to me. But I felt like if it weren't now, it would undoubtedly be never. There are contingent events or surprises in all of our lives that can alter both our direction and our possibilities. Most of the time, we can only identify these when we look back into the past. I learned in life to anticipate and watch for contingent events that can bring both danger and opportunity. As Jude Wanniski says, "All growth, including political growth, is the result of risk-taking." The universe tends to oppose bold declarations, and the world wasn't going to throw me a ticker-tape parade in honor of my courage. It doesn't work that way. The first person, who wasn't celebrating, of course, was Mother. Even though I was successful, her mind went back to my accident. She immediately became terrified about my financial future, convinced I would end up broke and dependent on her.

I knew that the biggest obstacle to my new declaration would be breaking away from Cooke & Bieler. I was locked into both an employment contract and a non-compete agreement with the owners, although I wasn't leaving to compete against them. I was the largest revenue producer in the firm, had the heaviest client load, and the largest share of the fees compared to any other partners. They were not happy at all. For them, my exit was a bolt from the blue. I'd shaken up their world with no warning. There was anger ("Who do you think you are anyway?"). There was self-righteousness ("How dare you, you have a contract!") and other completely normal emotions for such a situation. When one person makes a dramatic life shift, the effects ripple out to shake up others involved. These ripples do not make one party right and the other wrong.

I refused to reverse my decision, but I made a deal with Cooke & Bieler to leave without making it a matter of public record. I agreed to honor my non-compete in the investment business completely. In the end, my huge shift happened with a whisper. I did not leave for the same life with a competitor, but a different life altogether.

I broke free and headed West, like early American pioneers. Like them, I was declaring what I would not tolerate. But Like me, they weren't interested in sticking around back East. The vast majority didn't move for gold; they moved for a better life. They were restless for change, freedom, and new opportunities. So was I.

Beyond shifting my job and geography, the massive narrative shift from Cooke & Bieler to Silicon Valley shifted my habits, outlook on life, and even my social friends. The most significant, most effective shifts in life do that—it's never just about the decision. When a shift is tectonic (vs. the minor tremors of life changes), your entire ecosystem changes, and nothing looks like it used to.

Leaving Cooke & Bieler in the late 1980s was the last time in my life in which I had a regular paycheck. There were times I would miss that. I was about to be involved in creating the wrong product, in the wrong place, at the wrong time. It would come to be called "Nazi-Ware."

SOFTWARE FAIL

We learn more from our failures than from our victories.
—Russell Redenbaugh

I now found myself as CEO of Action Technologies, a Silicon Valley software company. Settling into my glass-walled corner office, overlooking other hungry, young technology startups, I wondered if I was born to innovate after all.

We worked in a rarefied environment at Action Technologies with top PhDs in Computer Science, including Terry Winograd. Terry was a full professor at Stanford at twenty-four years old. I was co-inventor on two of our patents. The new situation initiated me into a membership club of technological geniuses. It was a miracle that they'd have me.

Our product, a combination of project management and email, was very far ahead of its time. Email is ancient technology now, but it was rare in the 1980s, and to most people in business, a mystery. Email had been around longer for larger entities like the government and university systems on large mainframes. It was not common to have personal email on a personal computer.

For the most part, the people of corporate America were still photocopying memos and sending faxes. They were still picking up landlines to reach out and touch someone. Email existed on large mainframes used by universities and the government, but it was not common to have personal email on a personal computer. To most people in business, email was a mystery. AOL had only just appeared, and we were all getting used to their now historical "You've got mail!" announcement. Yahoo! was so new that people were still figuring out how to categorize it. Was it a search engine portal or some type of low-grade email? The Internet was in its infancy, and its customers were taking baby steps. They were hugging the couch, trying not to fall, and trying to navigate unfamiliar territory.

So we decided to fly a complicated time machine right through the center of Silicon Valley. As it turns out, this wasn't the smartest business idea. There's a difference between being ahead of your time and being so far ahead that people have no idea what you're talking about.

Our product was very complicated and sophisticated. It was a DOS product because Microsoft Windows wasn't out yet. It emulated Windows years before that interface came out. It was way ahead of the curve.

It was ahead of its time, but it was also the wrong product for that time's people and processes. Our software was a combination of email and project management. The software tracked requests, promises, and completions within a company. You could create and sort a database based on what deadlines and tasks were coming up, what was overdue, and by how much. You could slice it up in many different ways based on the information you were looking for. It performed these tasks very vigorously. So much, so that one of our critics called it, as noted, "Nazi-ware." Alienating users, of course, was not our intent.

The software tried to fix flaws in human nature. Only a small percentage of people have excellent practices for managing their commitments, deadlines, emails, and follow-through. The idea with this product was that you didn't need to be perfect in your methods. If you used this software, it would guide you into tracking commitments that you made to people and vice versa. As far as we were concerned, it fixed the procrastination error in human mental software.

People didn't like it. OK, people **hated** it! One of many things I learned from the experience is how much people loathe saying "I promise" about anything. You can have the world's best, most airtight systems in place, but as long as humans are around, there is always the possibility of things going off the rails.

The unfortunate part, especially for our investors and our financials, was that we were all true believers. We were drinking the Kool-Aid by the gallon. We thought this was the most incredible product in the entire Bay Area, if not the world. Looking back, the reason we thought this was because we were all the kind of people who didn't need this software. It was the disorganized masses we were out to save.

Unlike the fast burn of the gunpowder in my homemade rocket, failure is a slow burn. Success and failure do generally not happen overnight. While the developers improved the product and the sales guys peddled it to corporations, it was my job as CEO to raise the money to keep us all in business.

I raised money in two different rounds, selling shares to angel investors and doing whatever else I could to bring in funding. Nothing was working.

Then I found a friend and professional investor, Bill Welty, to put in money and join our board. He quit his professional investing job and became a full-time executive. The truth was self-evident, and everyone agreed when I recommended that we find somebody better at being a software CEO than me. I quit and stayed on the board. Several years later, the company went down swinging into the Silicon Valley graveyard of failed startups.

It was a considerable risk, leaving the financial and career security of Cooke & Bieler for the fast-paced excitement of Silicon Valley. There were times when I thought the decision was a mistake, walking away from the financial world's money and security. But it was not a mistake. There are few lessons in easy victories. Little did I know that one of my next significant accomplishments would be won not on the corporate battlefield but mano a mano using my body and my wits. I would develop expert knowledge of hand-to-hand combat techniques. I was about to stun sighted fighters by proving beyond question that I was one of the best in the world.

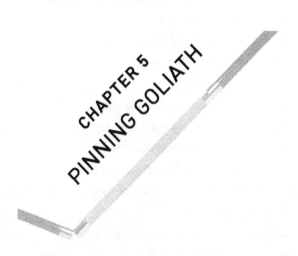

CHAPTER 5
PINNING GOLIATH

Periodically I discovered other narratives I wanted to shift. Shifting stories meant new declarations and actions needed to make these shifts. From the shock of blindness, the climb out of welfare, working at Cooke & Bieler, and then in Silicon Valley finally returning to the investment advisory business—the next significant shift that I would make was a personal, not professional one.

One day, when I was working out at the gym with my fitness coach, Steve Maxwell, he said, "Russell, I have a plan for you. I want you to become my client. I know you go to work early, so I'll come by at 5:30 every morning, and we'll go for a jog. Then we'll end up back at the gym, lift some weights, and then I'll bring you back home so you can get showered up and go to work."

I absorbed all this and realized something.

"Wait a minute, Steve. You're not offering to become my fitness coach. You're trying to change my whole life!" I said.

"You've got it," he said, "that's exactly right."

He was so disarmingly honest about it.

I said, "OK, sign me up."

After being his fitness student for a decade, at the age of fifty, Steve convinced me to try Jiu-jitsu. Jiu-jitsu is a ground fighting art that focuses on techniques and maneuvers with the hands and feet. A smaller, weaker person can overcome a larger, stronger one with Jiu-Jitsu. Jiu-jitsu is a sport where David can overtake Goliath using leverage and strategy, no slingshot required.

I reluctantly took a group class in Brazilian Jiu-jitsu

Steve was right. I loved it! Jiu-jitsu is strategy over strength, skill oversize; it's three-dimensional physical chess.

Grappling was a good fit for me, as I was never the athletic kid. I was always picked last for teams. Little League at the time had major and minor leagues. I didn't even make it into the minor leagues. I was energetic and fit, not a slob, but not well-coordinated and not a fighter. So I was bullied, which ingrained in me the instinct to back away in confrontational situations. I tried to open the distance between the bully and myself. Flight is most people's natural response; extend the distance, not close it.

In some martial arts and fighting sports, closing the distance is the exact correct action. For instance, when the fighters are "in a clinch" (which looks more like they're hugging), they can do almost no damage in boxing. They can't throw a punch and put their weight behind it because they're too close. In karate, if you're too close, you can't successfully kick your opponent. You need a certain amount of space; otherwise, all you can do is step on his toes or kick him in the shins. So the natural tendency is to open the distance, to allow space to strike.

In Jiu-jitsu, the most successful strategies involve doing the opposite of your instinctive reaction. **Moving against your emotions is also what is required to be a successful investor.** In Jiu-jitsu, by grappling, you reduce your opponent's capacity for punching and kicking. At the same time, you increase your capacity for throws, joint locks, and chokes to bring them to submission.

Hold the opponent close with one hand…
Quick squat down with the other hand…
Ankle pick…
Stand up quickly…
Step back with one hand still on his chest…
Push forward!
The opponent goes down.

It's inevitable. Under the laws of physics, if your opponent is on one leg, his torso is moving backward, and his leg that you're holding is moving forward, he will fall onto his back. These are all things that I learned, and it made perfect sense to me. Jiu-jitsu went completely against "normal" thinking. This reinforced for me how success often requires overcoming your instincts, fears, reactions, and prejudices. **It is overcoming your false common sense.** It's about shifting out of autopilot into discomfort, settling there, and being open to the possibility that the first action you feel like you should take might not be the right action. It might be correct, and it might be wrong; be open to the possibility either way. Shifting your narrative requires a willingness to be incorrect. The training in Jiu-jitsu gave me such physical confidence. It changed how I related to the world, both on the street and in the boardroom.

There were ten to twenty-five people in each class, mostly male, in their twenties and thirties, and all sighted with full use of their bodies. Most had taken up the art as a form of self-defense. Despite my limitations, I became very good at Jiu-jitsu. I was already fit and strong from a decade of training with Steve. I have to confess that it was very satisfying to beat up on those young kids as an older "handicapped" guy. David versus Goliath.

More so than my eyesight, the bigger problem was my hands. I don't have any grip with my left hand and a very modest grip with my right. So I would fight on my back, mostly using my feet and legs. This strategy works well with Jiu-jitsu since it's a non-striking martial art like judo or wrestling; no kicking or punching your opponent. Once again, Steve was right, and it fits me perfectly.

The lesson here is about playing your own game rather than trying to win someone else's strategy or succeed in someone else's narrative.

David changed the rules completely. He had no armor, nothing to limit his movement, and he fought from a great distance. The six-foot-seven giant used hand-to-hand combat, fighting up close to win his game. With his slingshot and pebble, David never got in range and essentially became the world's first sniper. Play your own game, no matter how big the competition is or how unlikely it seems that you will win.

After it was clear that I had some talent, Steve had another big idea: I should start competing. After winning several smaller, regional competitions, I competed at the nationals in California and won. Steve and my other coaches encouraged me to go to the world championship in Rio de Janeiro, Brazil.

Walking into the Brazilian arena was overwhelming. It was huge, confusing, and impossible to hear. The Seattle Seahawks NFL team calls their fans "the twelfth man on the field" because their stadium amplifies noise. I was now to play my game in the middle of that chaos. Standing in the center of it all, I was scared to death and promptly made it to the restroom in time to be sick.

Six fights run simultaneously, resulting in the screaming echoes of fans cheering, coaches shouting, and bodies slapping onto mats. Nobody can hear a thing, including the competitors. I was now fighting blind and deaf. When a blind man cannot hear, he cannot see.

Nearing the end of my match, I was exhausted and on the brink of giving up. My arms and legs felt like a thousand pounds, and the noise had created a ringing in my ears. I became disoriented, discouraged, and was seconds away from quitting. Then, through the din, I heard the voice of my Brazilian coach Solo Ravera, black belt, ten-time Jiu-jitsu World Champion. He was yelling something at me. I forced my mind to clear the ringing in my ears to make out what he was saying.

"No, don't give up Russell, if you could only see his face! You've got him! Push it!"

I don't know how, but I found some reserves, pushed through, got him in a chokehold, and choked him out. Star Trek fans might recognize the result as similar to the Vulcan nerve pinch where the blood supply to the head is cut off by pressing critical blood vessels in the neck.

To my incredible surprise, I won the championship.

Most people give up just when they're about to achieve success. They quit on the one-yard line. They give up at the last minute of the game one foot from a winning touchdown.

—Ross Perot

I kept winning outside the arena in Rio! I developed a following and became a local celebrity. Kids started following me around wherever I went. I didn't know what to make of this and was bemused.

After winning that initial gold medal, I went back and won two more golds in my weight division to make sure it wasn't just luck. I also won two silvers and a bronze in the unlimited weight division, where it indeed was David versus Goliath. My opponents, of course, had a disadvantage: they could see. I learned an essential lesson in Jujitsu, applicable to much of life. Winning is much easier when your opponent underestimates you. To quote the great military leader of Chinese antiquity, Sun Tzu: "If your opponent is of choleric temper, seek to irritate him. Pretend to be weak, that he may grow arrogant."

Like wrestling, in Jiu-jitsu, you fight in your weight class, and that's where I was winning. In my last competition, I entered the unlimited weight division and fought against a huge guy, a real Goliath. When I entered the arena and walked onto the mat, the crowd recognized me from prior years, and I got an ovation. For once, I was not at all nervous and didn't get sick before the match. I had nothing to prove. I wasn't fighting for myself. My training partner later said he could tell by my posture that I'd already decided I was going to lose. My declaration at that moment was not to win but to avoid getting hurt.

I did, however, make Goliath go the distance. I didn't submit, and we went the full time of the match. He won on points and received quiet applause for his victory. I earned a thundering standing ovation for not giving up. Although second place is where the losing starts, it won me respect that Goliath did not achieve. Joining the Martial Arts Community also had another effect. Whenever you change your direction, you change your social network. When I entered Jiu-jitsu, I entered a new network of relationships.

POSTLUDE

In 2015 I gave a motivational talk at a local Jiu-jitsu event here in Northern California. After the talk, one of the audience members came up and introduced himself as a Jiu-jitsu coach named Henry. As it turns out, he was in Rio de Janeiro in 2005 and saw me in that last fight, when I won gold in my weight division but lost to Goliath in the unlimited weight division.

"You know Russell, whenever I think I'm up against something too hard in life, I think of you," he told me after my talk.

He added that whenever his students want to quit, he tells them my story. Then, he called over some of his students who were across the room to meet me.

"This is the guy I've been telling you all about," he told them. "This is the blind guy who won the gold and silver in Rio. This is him right here."

I felt humbled to play even a small role in inspiring others not to quit in the face of a challenge.

This role, of helping others lower the mental barriers of what they believe they can and cannot do, is one that has always come naturally to me. Naturally, however, doesn't always mean easy.

APRIL 2013

"What was I *thinking* when I said I would do this?"

My mind was racing with anxiety and thoughts of impending failure.

This could only end badly.

Standing in the stage wings in Bend, Oregon, with my guide dog at my side, I was about to deliver a TEDx Talk. The audience was entrepreneurially-minded individuals. They were looking to find inspiration and valuable messages from my life story. I thought they were crazy for even inviting me. On stage would be the first time I ever told my story publicly.

There had been many requests over the years, all of which I'd declined. This wasn't coming from a place of shyness, excessive humility, or any grandiose reason. I felt that the things that happened to me in my life were private, personal, not for public consumption, and unremarkable.

I was nervous about the precise timing of TEDx talks, eighteen minutes exactly. Would there be a large hook to remove my guide dog and me from the stage if I went over the allotted time?

I told my story with images of my large Mormon family and my hometown of Salt Lake City projected onto the screen behind me. My journey, as it turned out, was a story that people wanted to hear.

In addition to telling my personal story in that speech, I introduced an idea that has been a vital grounding principle in my life, especially when defying expectations and charting my course. **The picture I presented was of making declarations of what you are not willing to tolerate (for me, being dependent on others) as a route to gaining what you want in life. Most of those in the audience were used to hearing the reverse, the idea of creating a vision of what you do want and then going after it.** There's nothing wrong with positive declarations. I know it works for many people. I've found that declaring what you will not tolerate has worked very well for me, dating back to that day in the hospital after my final eye surgery.

At the TEDx Talk, I left it for each individual in the audience to decide what worked best for his or her life. And at the end of this book, when we part ways, I will leave you with that same choice. Whether you choose to shift or not shift your narrative is up to you.

Despite my apprehensions, people loved the talk. I think I even smiled. The audience gave me an enthusiastic response, a standing ovation.

That's when the thoughts started formulating in my mind. What if, beyond "amazing, wonderful, and fantastic," I could share my story even more in-depth? **What if I could shift the narrative of your life by teaching you to change your declarations and taking the right actions?** Was it possible that anything I had to say could move the needle in some way and create a shift in how people looked at the plotline of their lives? At the very least, I wanted to pose the question—is the narrative of your life working? Is it producing the results you want? Leaving the event that day, having rewritten a prior declaration that "my story is private and of no interest to anyone," the idea of this book was born. The core idea of how I shifted my narrative and how others can do the same. Learn my story and learn the critical elements of a narrative. Distinguish which narratives are limiting you. From there, you will remember the actions needed to shift them. Following the example of my life has the potential to transform yours. Using my model as a template is where the inspiration ends, and your work begins.

*Loss of vision did not deter
Russell's competitive nature.*

*Immersed in culture while visiting the home of a local
family inspired by Russell to start a school for blind and
disabled children in Jodpahur, India.*

Russell, competing in the BJJ Masters Seniors World Championship, earned three gold medals, two silvers, and one bronze, fighting sighted opponents.

Competition Strategies in Jiu-Jitsu: bait, hook, and remain one step ahead in the game.

The champion; standing high atop the medals platform at a Brazilian World Jiu-jitsu Championship.

*The Laffer Curve, Back-Of-The-Napkin Edition,
by Art Laffer*

*Three generations of Redenbaughs.
Russell is riding his father's antique
BMW with his son David.*

Russell fishing and youngest son Jamie. However, he could not see the outdoors. Russell instilled a love for it in his children.

Russell with granddaughter Isobel and guide dog Coulter.

After being declared blind and "handicapped" for life, Russell defied expectations from welfare to wealth, earning an MBA from Wharton and then becoming Chief Investment Officer at a prominent Philadelphia money management firm that he helped grow to $6 billion in assets.

Russell's enjoyment outdoors leads him to boating, camping, fishing, and waterskiing.

Russell served as one of eight Commissioners on the U.S. Civil Rights Commission in Washington D.C. under three Presidents: George, H. W. Bush, Bill Clinton, and George W. Bush.

President George H.W. Bush in the White House Rose Garden announced Russell's appointment to the United States Commission on Civil Rights. His guide dog, Royce, is by his side.

Russell doing show & tell at a local school where he told stories of being more in your life.

Russell with his first of three gold medals in the Brazilian jiu-jitsu world championships.

Russell and his youngest son Jamie carried the torch for the 2002 Winter Olympics in Salt Lake City.

Russell, daughter Allie, youngest son Jamie and an event planner as part of the 2002 Winter Olympics.

Parasailing in Bermuda, where Russell was attending an economic summit on tax policy and incentives.

"Mood is everything, and narratives are the rest."
—Russell Redenbaugh

In 2016, he was posing with tokens representing a lifetime of accomplishments.

Visiting Stonehenge in 2010, a site that resonates with Russell because of its permanent example of human achievement. We marvel at the declaration of Stonehenge without knowing the how or why

Russell teaching a child to read

Teaching the next generation to swim.

SECTION II
DRIFT

CHAPTER 6
WHAT YOU "KNOW"

F ollowing the accident, my physical conditions resulted in an agonizingly long purgatory. The doctors (along with my nervous mother) were concerned that the retina in my remaining eye would detach, leaving me blind if I moved too much. As it turns out, their many eye surgeries to fix it did this. Lying in limbo and waiting to know if I would be living in the sighted world or darkness was more debilitating than being blind. The indecision and inability to plan and move forward were depressing.

The final news of my blindness forced me to choose between the disabling stories the doctors, my mother, and society shared or a heroic tale filled with challenges and obstacles. That I was blind was out of my and the doctors' control, but I could choose how to deal with my circumstances. My father and I set about creating a story of challenge yet success. It was the classic choice: See the glass as half empty or half full.

My father and I chose half full. Not because we believed this, but because the glass half full story opened rather than closed opportunities.

This choice, as difficult as it seemed, was still a relief. Before my accident, I had been living my life as a typical sighted teenager. I may not have been a role model, but I acted like a normal kid. My accident made returning to normal impossible. The challenges seemed insurmountable. I could ignore those challenges as long as the doctors continued pursuing surgeries in the hope of saving my sight. But once it was clear nothing could be done to restore my sight, I had to choose how to live. My circumstances changed; I was now blind and would remain so. I would need to learn to see, act and be different in the world. I had a lot to learn.

My purgatory left me unable to act. Many of us have been paralyzed at one time or another, unable to function. I've observed another more common purgatory with which most of us are familiar. Lack of action is the purgatory of indecision, conflict, and suffering. A self-limiting story can cause failure to act. Many of us, consciously or unconsciously, live in a limiting narrative. Like a leaf in a stream, not examining your life, not taking responsibility results in you drifting through life. Limited narratives cause the drift that goes unconscious or unresolved, causing suffering. Is this you? Are you getting the results you want from your life? Are your narratives serving you?

NO QUICK FIXES

How is setting a new narrative course different from setting a goal? Let's talk about Steven Covey's S.M.A.R.T. Goals. A S.M.A.R.T. (specific, measurable, actionable, results-oriented, timely) goal is a type of declaration. A declaration is the starting point of a narrative. A declaration describes a specific purpose, is measurable, and requires action for it to be successful. I have nothing against S.M.A.R.T. goals; they're much better than stupid dreams. Mr. Covey has helped many people. He has organized goal setting in a way that is implementable in life, and I admire his work.

S.M.A.R.T. goals work well for motivated people who do not have disabling narratives. Take a moment to count how many people you know who don't have any story keeping them from moving forward.

The fact is, when it comes to life improvement or any type of solution, there are many paths to success. The limitation of S.M.A.R.T. goals and other one and done strategies is that they may not shift your life narrative.

But, if S.M.A.R.T. goals or other techniques are already working in your life, leading you to a narrative that works, you don't need to keep reading this book. If everything is fine and working out, please find one of the many people for whom other goal-setting systems have *not* worked, and give them your copy. It can't hurt to pay forward any solutions that make life work better, can it? If you're still reading, then perhaps you are living in a narrative that's holding you back. Maybe, long ago, you accepted a declaration (or many) assigned to you by your family, culture, church, country, or fill in the blank. And now those declarations have set the course to somewhere you didn't want to go. How would you feel about the opportunity to course-correct and create a narrative that takes you where you want to go?

I intend to present you with the options—shift your narrative or don't. The model I'm about to share with you, and the tools that go with it will support a shift. In short, you may *choose* your life narrative instead of living the one that you now find yourself in.

In the interactions we have with one another, we modify one another. We write our narratives with language, and as we interact with people, our language and narrative can change. We all see this when a child has a new school friend and immediately adopts the newfound companion's new speech pattern, attitudes, and values. As Nietzsche wrote, "And if you gaze long into an abyss, the abyss also gazes into you." Your narrative grows because similar supporting narratives reinforce it.

All human beings live in narratives; this is how we communicate and relate to others. We grow up with different stories about the world and ourselves. Suffering happens when we live in a dissatisfying story. Sometimes we live in conflicting narratives. Sometimes we live a story unrealized due to lack of action. Sometimes we act without connection to anything meaningful. All this produces suffering and a mood. These moods are symptoms of missing actions or stories and signal where to investigate further. Conflicting narratives such as "I am a vegan" and "I love Big Macs" will cause anxiety and suffering.

Furthermore, we reinforce narratives with the company we keep. Birds of a feather flock together. We tend to seek out people who are like ourselves, but the more time we spend *with* each other, the more similar we become. People connect, relate, and communicate through storytelling or narratives. Every day we share stories with others; we edit through selection or detail the stories we tell as our way to belong. "I'm a wine enthusiast" is something you might share with friends but not necessarily advertise with recovering alcoholics. Just as people try to match moods, they also choose and modify narratives to match the company they keep. In the interactions we have with one another, we modify one another. We write our narratives with language, and as we interact with people, our language and narrative can change. We all see this when a child has a new school friend and immediately adopts the newfound companion's new speech pattern, attitudes, and values. Your narrative grows because similar supporting narratives reinforce it.

Think of cable news. FOX, CNN, and MSNBC. Republicans watch FOX while Democrats watch MSNBC. Audiences seek out like-minded commentators for their information. Like-minded friends connect on social media; Facebook even has a "like" button on their site.

Are you living in an expired narrative? Are you mimicking the actions of those whose success you admire without a deep understanding behind those actions? A real shift cannot happen from the surface. A narrative change comes from the core.

Shifting the entire narrative of your life means going very deep and swapping out all the things that are not working. This is more effective than hoping for change. A vegan hot-dog-eating champion is stuck in two narratives that cannot coexist. This example may sound silly, but incompatible narratives often limit people.

Start with a declaration to end your conflict or suffering. If you have been dazed and confused, making such a declaration will change your mood. Then invent a narrative or story to try on, test, modify, and develop. If my declaration had been to go to Harvard Business School, my odds of success would be higher if I modified it. "Go to a top business school" would have been (and indeed was) an effective narrative. Move into action. Think about the simplest steps you can take and measure your results. Then make course corrections as needed. A holistic change of this kind is not the same as a simple goal like losing five pounds after the holidays. A well-stated declaration coupled with new actions or habits will produce much more of what you want. It will take a lot of time and effort. If it were easy, everybody would be doing it. James Clear says success is a lagging indicator of effective declarations and habits. The results of the habits can be measured, such as increased wealth or fitness over time.

Are you where you thought you'd end up? Or did something shift at some point, and you can't put your finger on what it was and when it happened? It was by a complex change that you arrived here, and that's what it will take to set a new course.

My habit of thinking about change helped transform me further. When I turned fifty, Steve Maxwell put me on the path of transformation. I went from a blind investment advisor working at a desk with limited use of my hands to a Brazilian Jiu-jitsu black belt. I was even a three-time world champion fighting sighted opponents.

Declarations are the first step toward shifting your narrative; they are the announcement of a new possibility. Declarations open new opportunities and close others. Sometimes a declaration states what you *don't* want or will *not* do.

UNEXAMINED ASSUMPTIONS

There are other paths that my Jiu-jitsu story could have taken. What if I believed that a blind person couldn't do Jiu-jitsu? Or I thought that I was too old to compete? Or I decided that my hands would prevent me from succeeding? Sometimes we consciously make declarations. But more often than not, many of our beliefs have existed for a long time. We've been walking through our lives with a specific set of unexamined assumptions. We make assumptions about ourselves, others, and life, in general, that limit us.

I guarantee you the majority of your assumptions are wrong. I promise you that the majority of those wrong assumptions are also unexamined. Over time assumptions become your reality.

Have you heard, "they say" or, "all the experts say"? Fill in the blank. "They" say a lot about the hole in the ozone layer, things that will give us cancer, or protecting your retirement fund with diversification. They say it, and without close examination of the facts, you believe it.

Money tends to be a magnet for unexamined assumptions. For some people, beliefs about people who have money can be crippling. What if you held the unexamined assumption that money is wrong? Would that mean that, therefore, if you have money, you must have done something terrible to get it? The idea that having money and being a humane, caring person cannot exist together seems to be common. We could call this the morality of poverty. People who believe that honest money only comes from hourly wages rarely have much of it. Someone with this narrative, for instance, would not want to own stocks. What if you could change your income by making a declaration coupled with action? Change your income by declaring that you will increase your value in the marketplace and taking action to make it so. The first step is to make a declaration of what you will and will not tolerate about money.

My journey has been from welfare to wealth because, for me, welfare was unacceptable. I also never thought of wealth as something evil or a value existing in contrast to being a virtuous person. If you live in a story, a narrative, where money is terrible, you are unlikely to have a lot of it because you are unlikely to take the actions needed to acquire it.

With these often-unexplored assumptions in place about money, the outcome of "being rich" is still coveted. It is a popular narrative. You turn on the television and watch *Entertainment Tonight* or another celebrity news show. You see the popular culture of flash, dash, and cash in story after story. It's exciting, sexy, and compelling; the expendable cash, red carpet, limousine lifestyle. Your imagination kicks in.

"Must be nice; I want that."

What is unseen on those shows is the amount of hard work, skill, and discipline it took to arrive on that red carpet. The money didn't fall from the sky. It took certain declarations and actions to create that narrative. A habit of hard work also applies to any of the other executives, bankers, sports figures, entrepreneurs, anyone you look at and say:

"Must be nice; I want that."

Powerful people make declarations about how much wealth they want to acquire. They determine which actions they are willing to take to achieve it day after day. The idea that money is evil is a pervasive and corrosive narrative. Negative declarations will have the opposite effect of those the wealthy make. If you tell yourself money is bad, people with money are bad; I don't deserve to keep it, etc.—there is a slim chance that the money will stay in your wallet.

Do you know what every lottery winner learns right away? They understand that their family is much larger than they thought. Third cousins, once removed, come out of the woodwork, hand extended for their piece of the pie. The outcome for the lottery winner, who did not take the usual steps it took to earn this windfall, is exceptionally disorienting. They are suddenly living in a dramatically different life narrative. As a result, many tend to lose their winnings and shift back to a more familiar but limiting narrative: We prefer a typical swamp to an unknown Camelot.

SEEKING NARRATIVES

Erik Weihenmayer, the only blind person ever to climb Mt. Everest, made an interesting observation on his way up. He said that on the road to Everest's peak, you find many more campers than climbers. They are dream tourists, making tracks through someone else's camp but not doing anything. They tell anyone who listens that they're going to be mountain climbers, but they're camping at the lower levels.

"Camping at the lower levels" happens in life off the mountain too. The billionaire investor Mark Cuban coined a term for people who aspire to become entrepreneurs but don't take the necessary actions, "wanna-preneurs." They know they don't want a "job," but they don't want to put in the work of building their own business from the ground up. They're camping on the lower mountain, hoping someone will come by and carry them up. They want the reward but without the work.

I'm sure if you survey any MBA class and ask, "Which of you want to be leaders?" every single hand will go up. Well, of course, I want to be a leader because that's the right answer. That's what I'm supposed to want to be. The automatic reaction is to raise their hands. Leaders have a profound responsibility to take care of the company's concerns and the lives of the people they lead. It's not an easy job. The MBA students chime in with only a shallow understanding of what it means to be a leader.

If you want to be successful, look at people who have positive, even radical narratives. Look at outside-the-box thinkers. Henry Ford didn't try to build cars by hand. Instead, he built a system of production. This system of production had to be preceded by a new narrative about how cars could be made. Steve Jobs didn't come to the computer hardware business through the normal channels. He credited a college calligraphy course as the important influence on the design of the Mac. What story is trapping you? What story will free you to move forward? That is the story you need. That is your new narrative.

CHAPTER 7
DEFINING NARRATIVES

WHAT IS A NARRATIVE?

A narrative is the kind of story that explains one's events and experiences, **whether real or not**. Through storytelling, human beings can observe, communicate and relate using language. It appears that we live in a world of objects, but in reality, we live in a world of distinctions. Truth, beauty, and honor are not things, a table is a thing, but it is only a table to a culture with the culture of using tables. It acquires its meaning only for those cultures that have the distinction "table." The culture/language is the way we make sense of the world in which we live. Our sense-making skill is a function of our particular cultural and personal histories. Our myths, our religions, **our narratives** are all part of that cultural and personal history. Part of what makes us human is language. The journey from complete helplessness to independence begins with language. Language allows us to couple, operate, and coordinate with other human beings. It is how we create societies. Language enables us to build narratives rich with opinions and facts. Philosophers call these assessments and assertions. We propel organization forward through interaction (promises, requests, offers, and commitments).

Narratives start with a declaration. President Kennedy historically declared that America would "put a man on the moon and bring him back alive in this decade." What followed were all the conversations and actions needed to make that happen. Americans adopted a narrative about the US landing on the moon. The government launched discussions in science, finance, and policy. Reports across the country changed as everyone saw space travel as a possibility. Americans were now part of the Space Race. Nationwide pride swelled as space travel became part of the American story. The Russians seemed to be winning the space race in the 1950s. As Tom Wolfe wrote in *The Right Stuff*: "The men chosen for this historic mission [space flight] took on the archaic mantles of the single-combat warriors of a long-since-forgotten time. They would not be going into space to do actual combat ... [but] they were risking their lives for their country, for their people, in 'the fateful testing,'"

For Kennedy's declaration to come to pass, America would create NASA, fund it, staff it, and do the needed research. For at least ten years, making the space program part of our national narrative was essential. We were going to the moon. The media covered it all, from tragedies to triumphs. America cheered on the astronauts and scientists who were making it happen.

In *The Right Stuff*, a scene reveals the importance of the national narrative and dreams ignited by Kennedy's declaration. NASA scientists and astronauts argue whether the hatch on the Mercury 7 space capsule needs explosive bolts. With such bolts, astronauts can open the door themselves in case of an emergency. The scientists insist that this is the final version of the space capsule and refuse to make changes. The test pilots square up, look the scientists in the eyes, and remind them what fuels the space program (and their jobs).

Pilot Gordon Cooper says to the scientists, "Do you boys know what makes this bird go up? Funding makes this bird go up."

Gus Grissom backs him, saying, "That's right. No bucks, No Buck Rogers."

The others chime in and make their point. "Without the safety of explosive bolts, we're not going." That also is a declaration.

Narratives are the connective tissues of the events of our lives. They are the stories we tell ourselves. We use them to identify with whom we wish to connect because the most profound human need is belonging.

EXAMPLES OF NARRATIVES

Parenting Success

Most have heard of Warren Buffett but not his older but junior partner Charlie Munger. Buffett is unlikely to leave a single dime of his billions to his two sons. Charlie Munger admits to being more patient than Warren. He said that if his heirs don't deserve the money, it will return to its rightful owners. If they don't know how to keep it, they won't.

I have seen heirs lose their inheritance many times. The relevant saying is "shirtsleeves to shirtsleeves in three generations." Rarely do children outperform their parents if the parents are top performers. Malcolm Gladwell makes this point in *Outliers*. The top performers on Wall Street and in law tend to come from lower-middle-class backgrounds. The ones that come from upper-class backgrounds can develop bad habits. Bad habits develop when parents use money to protect children from the consequences of foolish actions. When we interrupt the process of learning, we may end up with an entitled child. Privilege without responsibility is a formula for failure.

Yet, it is so tempting to try and protect our children from harm. Like so many others, I am guilty of this. I am a parent of three children, ranging in age from late twenties to early thirties. I named my youngest Jamie after the partner at Cooke & Bieler who hired me. Allie, my middle child, is adopted and most like me in personality. David is my oldest and named after my brother, whom you will learn about later in the book. David thinks most like me, but he has a better sense of humor!

I've learned over the years, often the hard way, that there are life experiences that you can't buy or bypass for your kids. They have to learn for themselves.

Some people call this tough love. It's beyond that. If you shield kids from any sort of danger, you're failing to let them see how the world works. You're setting them up for failure by telling them what gifted geniuses they are. You are not helping by telling them what special snowflakes they are and that everyone wins and that everyone gets a prize. Those of us in the real world know that to be untrue.

A relative has three children. They once came to stay with us at our home in Florida. One muggy Florida afternoon, Jared, the seven-year-old boy, guided me to the bank. I spotted a teachable moment. I can't resist teaching, especially when it comes to money matters.

"Jared," I asked him as we navigated down the bustling town street, "Where does money come from?"

"My mom and dad," he answered in kind of a "duh!" tone.

"Yes, but where do they get it?" I asked.

"Well, they go to work," he answered.

"Oh, so they do a job?" I asked.

"I guess," the boy responded.

"And how do banks make money?" I asked as we entered the chilly air-conditioned bank lobby from the furnace outside.

"They hold your money," Jared said.

"Yes, that's what they do, but how do they MAKE money?" I pressed.

"Well," he said, "I'm not sure, but they must do some job."

That's when the idea of the "job jar" was born. I wanted to teach a lesson about money. I wrote job names and how much the jobs paid on scraps of paper. I put the job scraps in an empty peanut butter jar. The jobs were folding laundry, washing dishes, picking up dog poop, and so on. When any of the three kids wanted money, we told them to reach into the job jar and fish out a job. So, when a kid came and begged for money for candy or comic books, we said, "No, because how does money happen?" and the kid would remember, "Ohhhh, the job jar," and hurry off to select a job to do. From then on, whenever the kids would visit, I would pull out the job jar. Everyone would work to exchange money for jobs. Later on, Jared and his brother, Alex, made $200 shoveling snow in Boston; this was a lot of money for kids their age.

We also took the kids to a kids' resort called Wannado City. The resort used their own currency, nothing from the U.S. Mint. To spend Wannado money, you need to earn it. Like the job jar, kids can pick the jobs they want to do. Jared's brother, Alex, and baby sister, Lydia, chose to be firemen. They gave them little fireman suits, trained them about the job, and gave them a fake fire to put out. Firefighting earned them money needed to buy a slice of pizza for lunch. The kids learned from the job jar and Wannado City to earn money from work. They stopped asking for it from Mom, Dad, Uncle Russell, the bank, or an ATM. There's a certain percentage of the population today who could benefit from a trip to Wannado City.

Lecturing your kids about money is not as effective as helping them build sound habits. Teach them actionable financial narratives. Teach them useful information, don't preach to them. Invent games like the job jar! Make learning and shifting narratives fun and meaningful! Unfortunately, I learned this lesson too late for my children, but I'm passing it on.

Unicorns

The investment and economics industries are composed of people with narratives. Many such narratives are deeply flawed. Some of the narratives are no longer true today if they were ever confirmed.

One standard Wall Street narrative is true believer seeking unicorns and Cinderellas. Many investment professionals try finding Princesses disguised as scullery maids. Naturally, Wall Street true believers find more Cinderella stocks than exist. Their narrative about the importance of finding the next Apple or Google informs advice to clients. This advice is often detrimental to the client's bottom line.

Another wrong Wall Street narrative is that diversification will protect you. The theory is that since different assets are uncorrelated, owning some of everything can offset risks. But when a crisis happens, there is, in effect, a giant margin call on all assets. Correlations between asset classes (gold, stocks) disappear as they are all sold for cash. My business partner James wrote in a recent edition of our newsletter, *Policy-Based Investing,* "The last three years, like other periods in history, are a clear example that diversification is a 'fool's game' in that it allows one to reach mediocre results from whichever side one starts." We do not believe in diversified portfolios. Contrary to conventional wisdom, diversification is what you do when you don't know what to do."

The investment narrative that you should hold more bonds as you age is also wrong—holding bonds used to work when bond rates were high. The government is now artificially suppressing bond rates. AAA and government bonds may decline thirty to fifty percent when interest rates normalize higher. These are not the low-risk assets in which one near retirement should be investing.

James' and my role as investment advisory partners is to reveal how these dangerous narratives harm wealth. We help clients find more powerful narratives to protect and grow their capital. We believe that our report called *Policy-Based Investing*, where government economic policies determine asset prices is a more robust and lucrative story to invest within than commonly sold Wall Street myths that have failed time and again.

CHAPTER 8
THE STORY THAT FREES YOU

F ull disclosure—change is hard. A close colleague learned about the ten: ten rule working as a consultant for corporations like IBM and Applied Materials. Unless there's a ten times return, you're not going to get people to change more than ten percent.

We find a related concept in economist Daniel Kahneman's work on loss aversion. A loss is twice as painful as an equal size gain. If a coin toss results in a $100 loss or a $150 profit, most people *will not* take the bet. But if the coin toss will result in a $100 loss or a $200 gain, most people *will* take the bet. People avoid losses twice as much as they pursue profits in a risk-based situation. All human behavior has evolutionary roots. Perhaps loss aversion served a more explicit purpose when saber-toothed tigers abounded. But now, our loss aversion may stop us from changing our narratives. Your New Year's resolution to go to the gym daily often fails by February. The benefit is not at least twice as appealing as the pain and inconvenience.

I look on in amusement and a little pity at people who are on a lifelong search for the Holy Grail of self-improvement. They want entirely painless, risk-free, transformational "life change" pills. There is no Holy Grail. There is no return without risk and effort. I've studied both risks and returns from every possible angle. I repeat. There is no return without risk; there is no result without effort.

Ignore and avoid victims, magic pill seekers, and anyone else with a disabling narrative that stops them from succeeding. This book is about the possibilities for *your* life. This book is a fork in your road. As Yogi Berra said, "If you come to a fork in the road, take it." You can continue down the path that seems comfortable and may have some modest returns. Or you can venture down the other way, one of change and transformation. Change the declarations that have defined your life until this point. Take the right actions to support those declarations. Free yourself from a narrative that is not serving you and create one that will. You are in charge here.

REWRITING THE STORY

When and why do we rewrite stories? When we realize the story of our life so far does not determine our future narrative. When we have conflicting narratives that do not allow consistent action. The vegan barbeque chef is going to have to choose to resolve inner conflict.

Rewriting your narrative takes courage and may be difficult and painful. It involves self-reflection. It requires admitting to yourself that some of your stories may be faulty. The Oscar-winning film *Good Will Hunting* is the story of conflicting narratives. The title character is a victim of childhood abuse and a stand-up blue-collar guy from Southie. He is also a self-taught mathematical genius with almost incalculable potential. As the story unfolds, we see the influences pulling him towards different narratives. There are the lifelong friends to whom he feels affinity and loyalty. As his psychologist notes, "Those guys would take a bat to your head for him." A different group of people, academics, see Will's vast potential. They want him to accept a job with a think tank or the NSA.

The people you surround yourself with will influence the story you tell yourself. The film seems to be a story of two competing narratives (with a romantic sub-plot). Will has been developing world-class academic skills while living a blue-collar life. The two competing narratives cause conflict as word of his genius leaks out. Harvard mathematicians are soon obsessing on putting Will in the "right" situation. The NSA wants to give him a job code-breaking. Will tells the men in suits where to go and returns to his job at a construction site. The clash between narratives, working-class versus Ivy League, cannot be integrated. Will feels safer and more comfortable with his buddies in their working-class story. The working-class Southie lifestyle is all he has known.

Underpinning the film is another more powerful narrative that informs Will's choices. Will falls for a girl, but he is afraid to love because he fears rejection due to childhood abuse. Will's core narratives are "I am not good enough" and "All the bad things that happened to me are my fault." Much of the movie is explicitly about rewriting narratives in the form of therapy. Will's Psychologist shakes him out of his narrative stupor. He explicitly states, "It is not your fault."

Will writes a new narrative with some help from his best friend, who threatened to kill Will if he is still a working-class nobody in 20 years. Most people don't have a friend, played by Ben Affleck, with the character to encourage them to make such a life-changing shift. He rejects both the working-class and Ivy League and drives California to get the girl and embrace love. It is a very Hollywood ending and also one of the most explicit treatments of narratives ever made. The new narrative of embracing love and being "good enough" does not prevent Will from becoming a successful professional in the future. It does not hurt that the love interest is a med student with a bright future. Will is starting to surround himself with people who will support his narrative of "you can be more."

SHIFTING NARRATIVES

It was 1988; South Korea was hosting the Olympic Games. In the States, the photo giant, Kodak, was in its prime, employing 145,000 people. The company's success was primarily due to public demand for photographic film and paper (remember that stuff you had to take to a shop to get developed before digital cameras were invented?).

I was on an airplane, commuting between Philadelphia and Silicon Valley. At that time, I flew many times a month. I was sitting in first class next to a man on his way to South Korea's Olympics. He worked for Eastman Kodak. At the time, they saw seventy percent gross margins in film sales. But digital photography was on the horizon. Working in technology, I saw how digital was catching on. I was eager to get his point of view when I found out he worked in the emerging digital division of Kodak.

"What are your plans for digital photography?" I asked him.

"We're not focusing much on digital," he admitted. "We don't see it as an alternative to film at all. The quality is so terrible it's a non-issue."

"Well, how many Moore's Laws doubling cycles will it take until the quality is good enough to take over a big part of your market?" I asked him.

Moore's Law[1] refers to an observation made in 1965 by Gordon Moore, the Intel co-founder. He saw that computer power had doubled every 18 months since the dawn of integrated circuits. He then predicted that the trend would continue.

---

1   https://www.webopedia.com/definitions/moores/

Moore's Law had not occurred to my seatmate, the Kodak executive from the digital division.

"Well, I never even thought about it that way," he said. He paused before continuing. "But I still don't think it [digital] is going to be a problem for us because the quality isn't there."

He was right at the time.

In 1999 George Lucas changed the film landscape. He shot *Star Wars Episode I: The Phantom Menace* mostly on digital. The Kodak executive was correct about digital photography for the moment. But he should have been very worried, especially since a large component of Kodak's business was commercial 70mm film cameras.

Unfortunately for Kodak, Moore's Law of doubling continued on schedule. The quality of digital photography multiplied dramatically. Kodak didn't see it coming, or in my seatmate's words, "didn't see it as a big problem." They took action based on the assessment that digital film quality was low. They also assessed that it would not improve soon, which was wrong. Kodak had another big blind spot. They were mostly focused on the high-end photography market. They missed the most significant part of their market. This was family photos developed at Kodak photo kiosks. For families, even less-than-perfect digital quality would be acceptable. Kodak had a narrative that caused them to miss how important speed and convenience would become.

Kodak was a victim of a strong institutional narrative developed over 100 years. The year I spoke with the exec on the plane was the company's 100th anniversary, 1988. They were dominant throughout the 20th century and "Kodak Moment" entered the lexicon. Kodak at the time had much of the information they needed to predict trends. At the very least, they should have been monitoring trends in digital photography. The Fuji DSP-1 came out the same year I spoke with the Kodak exec. It already had an impressive two megapixels of memory. With Moore's law in mind, they should have seen that by 2000, the two-year doubling would produce a 64X increase in memory and power. By the mid to late 1990s, digital cameras were widely available to the public. Absent the needed narrative shift, Kodak hurtled towards irrelevancy,

The company started losing power long before realizing it and long before the losses showed up in its financials. They continued to ignore the threat on the horizon.

Kodak's inability to speculate about the future cost them the company. In 2012 they filed for Chapter 11 bankruptcy protection and then announced the end of digital cameras and similar products. By the end of that year, they sold every division except motion picture film. In 2013 Kodak sold many of its patents to Apple, Google, Facebook, Amazon, and Microsoft.

Another example of costly corporate blindness is the reaction to Sean Fanning's Napster. It was the first digital music download service. Napster's primary use was piracy. Soon the music industry decided to start suing teenagers for illegal downloads. Taking teenagers to court was not a winning strategy for making money, nor could it curb what soon became rampant downloading of music. The authorities could not put the genie back in the bottle.

A new question emerged for the music industry. How are we going to prevent the unpreventable? Enter Steve Jobs, who understood intellectual property because of his company, Pixar. He also had a little computer hardware and software company called Apple. He said, "Look, you're not going to make as much money, but the way you're doing it now, the record stores are going to go broke. You need to get with the program, or you will also go out of business."

He promised to protect the value of copyrighted material. Making money from digital downloads was the best deal the record industry was going to get. They already knew suing teens and college kids was a losing battle. Times had changed. The way that music companies produced products had also changed. Creating, shipping and stocking hard media was much more expensive than moving data. Moving data vs. stuff is far more efficient; it's bits vs. atoms.

The writing was on the wall. Physical recording was becoming a costly dinosaur that nobody wanted to manage anymore. Unlike Kodak, the record companies and artists knew that they needed different actions to survive. In a way, Steve Jobs forced the music industry to adapt to new conditions. They took the deal to their credit, and today people go to places like iTunes for their music.

The wrong narrative can have severe, even dire consequences. In business, it can be deadly. Kodak's failure to shift moved them from dominant to an afterthought. Naturally, examples like these have continued, year after year. For example, Blockbuster failed because they were in denial about the cost of bandwidth. It had always been expensive and scarce. They assumed bandwidth would continue to be insufficient to stream and download movies. They missed what George Gilder in his book *Telecosm* described as "the thousandfold cost cliff that bandwidth would soon fall down." That means the cost of moving data would fall by a factor of 1000. There are dramatic hidden costs of not shifting your narrative, much as we see with newspaper classified ads. You do not just cost yourself at the corporate level, but now you're affecting other people's lives.

Many companies and industries have missed the narrative shift from moving atoms to moving bits. There is no more distance in long distance.

IMAGINE A NEW NARRATIVE

In the Stephen King novel, *Duma Key,* Edgar Freemantle said, "God punishes us for that which we cannot imagine." Every narrative shift begins as an exercise in imagination. Will Hunting was trapped in purgatory until he imagined a new future.

Fiction authors and screenwriters determine how their character will behave. They imbue them with goals and motivations. This is called "character development" and fits within "narrative structure." Consider a character named Bob. He is the main character in a romantic comedy about getting the girl of his dreams. When developing Bob's character, the writer will establish what the character is and is not. The writer will decide what Bob would and would not do in any given circumstance. The character Bob has established a declaration in his story: get the girl. His narrative is the story of what he will and will not do and how he will live his life on the journey of getting the girl.

Planning actions that support your declarations are crucial to living your narrative. Once you understand this, you can anticipate how you will handle various situations. You will not have to stop in each new situation and decide.

You are doing this all the time without even realizing it. It's tough for people to take actions that are inconsistent with their narrative. Do you know the narrative from which you are working? When you take action, do you always know why? Bob knows because the screenwriter dictates his actions, but who's dictating yours?

If you can't first imagine something, perhaps it's because nobody ever brought it up to you as a possibility. If you're poor and everybody you know is lacking, then there is no new movie plotline to go after. If you can't imagine being anything other than poor, you will likely stay poor. Shifting your narrative means writing a new story of what can and cannot exist. You can be the author of your history.

What if you could somehow imagine that you could move away from being poor through some set of actions? Imagination would open up a new set of possibilities to take those actions and produce results. We move through the world, imagining future action and shifting our narratives to align with them or carry on as usual. The bottom line is, if you can't first imagine something as a possibility for your life, then it's unlikely it will ever happen. Imagining is not nearly enough; it must be translated into declarations and actions. Imagination is the first step.

BEING MORE

I met Charles at our "Max-ercise" personal training sessions twenty years ago. It was around the time I got into Jiu-jitsu. He was working as a field technician for IBM. In talking with Charles, it became clear that the view he had of possibilities for his career and life was pretty limited. He was a knowledgeable, capable, skilled guy with an engineering degree. But his narrative seemed to be "this is it for me." He had a visible lack of enthusiasm for what he considered to be a dead-end job. He did not tell me this directly, but the message that I heard by listening between the lines was clear. I frequently listen between the lines—for me, a different kind of "seeing."

After Jiu-jitsu one night, he came back to our house to visit. Over the kitchen table, I started talking to him about ambition.

"Ambition?" Charles asked, sounding confused.

"Yes, ambition. Here's the deal, Charles, I'm blind; you're black. It is what it is. But WE CAN ALWAYS BE MORE."

We kept talking about ambition and "being more." We discussed making a new narrative for his life. I told him that, "All stories may be equally valid, but not all stories are equally powerful." The idea of stories of different power inspired Charles to craft a more powerful life story for himself. He began to build a new narrative where he would be a lifetime learner, open to seeing and creating new possibilities. He took ownership of where he was in life without blaming anyone else and then put a plan in action to create a new narrative of "being more."

Charles's actions centered on two areas, distinguishing between facts and opinions, also known as assertions and assessments. And a greater skill in understanding the difference between requests and offers. People's income goes up when they become better at distinguishing between these two things. Most organizations survive through making offers, not requests. Ford offering a zero down car loan is not a request.

Charles also picked up on my assertion that there are no problems. There is only what happened, what's missing, and what the next action is. Another action for him was to take business courses to expand his career options.

Charles emailed me recently, sharing how his life has changed.

"Russell, you killed the victim mindset in me. Today, it is supremely satisfying to live out of this new narrative of "being more"—my new life story. The declarations, narratives, and actions that you taught me, Russell, have given me a competitive advantage that helped me move from field technician into a successful management career and finally into a sales role at IBM."

He changed his narrative and then put himself into different actions.

Charles is not unique or unusual in his capacity to shift his narrative and change his life. Nor am I. Most people view my rise from blindness and welfare to success as something remarkable, even unreal. Life for me was ordinary. I changed. Change is available to you as well. Enough theory. Let's take action!

SECTION III
SHIFT

Your beliefs become your thoughts; Your thoughts become your words, Your words become your actions, Your actions become your habits, Your habits become your values, Your values become your destiny.

—**Mahatma Gandhi**

CHAPTER 9
STATES OF MIND

Mood is everything, and narratives are the rest.
—Russell Redenbaugh

A couple of hundred adult students sat in a West Coast auditorium waiting to hear me speak about state of mind. I would be telling them state of mind can shift your narrative either for better or for worse. My assistant and I even had the idea of making three-inch buttons with one of my most used "Russell-isms." "Mood is everything, and narratives are the rest." I used the word "mood" in the sense of "a receptive state of mind predisposing to action// was not in a giving *mood* at the time:" *Webster's.* The students were eager to hear my words of wisdom on how to improve their state of mind. They wanted to move into productive action and shift their narrative for the better.

The problem was, standing there backstage; I was in a nasty mood. I was back in my hotel room only thirty minutes before on a very unpleasant phone call with my wife. We were divorcing, which put me in a poor state of mind. My assistant tried to cheer me up. He even went so far as to slap me across the face, like in the movies. I wasn't at all interested in talking to this audience, with their big "Mood" buttons, about how to be in a good state of mind. Even as my guide dog started leading me out, I had no idea what I would tell them. I stepped into the center of the stage and adjusted my lapel mic.

"Mood is everything," I started, "and I am in a terrible mood right now. I just got off the phone with my wife. She and I are in the middle of a very unpleasant divorce."

That got a laugh. I was encouraged.

"Oh, I see some of you have been divorced, and others of you are thinking about it," I said.

That got an even bigger laugh. My state of mind began to improve. Learning can only happen in certain states of mind, and focused is one of them. My students (and I) were now ready to learn.

ON DEFEAT

> *Success takes a decade; failure can happen sooner.*
> —**Russell Redenbaugh**

There are no lessons in victories. A defeat contains many.

I'm a person who hates to lose—it's almost unbearable to me. But the reality of life, as we all know, is that defeat happens.

What do you do when there is such a defeat? How do you keep your narrative on track and keep pushing forward? It would be wrong for me to say: oh, just shift your narrative, suck it up and move on. Failure can be a devastating blow. But to win, you must handle the defeats, the losses, the depression, despair, and heartbreaks.

I don't always win; no one does. At times I am crushed and need to recover my state of mind slowly. It's not easy to bounce back. Just like anyone else, I am guilty of failing to shift my narrative, slumping down, and giving in to failure. One of the things that I'm still learning after all these years is how to pick my battles. I'm still learning every single thing that I'm writing about in this book. We are learning together.

You teach that which you most need to learn.
—**Russell Redenbaugh**

ACTIONABLE STATES OF MINDS

Moving from inaction to action always improves your state of mind. The entire spectrum of perspectives is from either taking productive action or not. Action is causal. The paralysis of indecision can produce a disabling, lousy state of mind.

Some actions cannot happen if a particular state of mind possesses you. An irritable, depressed, or angry state of mind, for instance, rarely leads to productive action.

Think of a state of mind as a conversation with yourself. A depressed state of mind centers around the notion that "life is messed up." And if that is my state of mind, I find the evidence to prove it everywhere I look. When there is no point in doing anything, "I might as well go back to bed."

The good news is, changing the conversation and shifting your mood is a straightforward process. The shift starts with awareness that your current mindset is not productive. Understanding and changing attitudes is a critical lesson. Identifying your perspectives is where the diagnosis begins. Follow the suffering.

I often use "mood reset" when this is the case. If the state of mind in a meeting is off for whatever reason, I bring the meeting to an abrupt halt and then take specific actions to reset the room's mood. I realize that we will accomplish nothing productive, so what is the point of moving on? Sometimes the resets involve playing certain music (appropriate to the age and group of people in the room). Other times I will shift the conversation's language. Successful motivational speakers like Tony Robbins and television evangelists are masters at this.

In small-group brainstorming sessions, an open-minded state of mind is essential. There are two parts to a brainstorming session. In the first, we put up all ideas, including goofy ones, without judgment. In the second part, we shift to critique. It is a different mood. Even the goofy ideas have the potential to trigger good ones. That is why it is essential not to quash those ideas in the first phase of brainstorming.

Companies brought in my friend Drew Lebby to change the culture. In a sense, he is a company doctor, which is tough. It is particularly tough when the company narrative is: "we've always done it this way." The correct response to "We've always done it this way" is, "Well, unfortunately, the rest of the world doesn't care that you think that. Your competition will be delighted that you continue to do what doesn't work."

Once I brought Drew into a company that I was consulting with. It was a well-known multi-billion-dollar agricultural concern. This was a family-owned business with third-generation owners who kept repeating, "It worked this way for my grandfather."

We gathered the top executives, seven of them, in the conference room. Drew, my friend, covered all the walls with butcher paper. He then handed the executives markers and had each of them write out the company history from their perspective. They all walked around the room and agreed on the story of the company's history.

Drew posed the question, for each key piece of history, "What were the circumstances that made that the right action at the time?"

He shifted the mindset from "we can't change because we haven't" to a state of mind of speculation, thinking about the future instead of the past. As a result of this openness, the group finally realized that business conditions are different now than in the past. They became open to new actions to address the new circumstances.

Finding a good mentor also requires a specific state of mind. You have to know you don't know everything or are unlikely to retain a good mentor. The need to be open is especially true if what someone tells you is contrary to your experience. To see results, you must have a state of mind of openness, willingness to speculate, and trust in the teacher.

There must be the open-mindedness to say, "I disagree with you, but I know you wouldn't deceive me. Tell me more. That's very different from my experience. Why do you say that?"

NARRATIVES AND STATES OF MIND

Narratives can shape states of mind, which are temporary. An improved state of mind can open possibilities for new actions. Ask yourself: In what state of mind do I find myself?

States of mind distort the world you see.

> "We don't see the world as it is; we see it as we are"
> **—Anaïs Nin**

Individual narratives are associated with specific states of mind. Anxiety, for example, arises when there is a mismatch between narrative and action. A vegan butcher is going to have to make a choice or will be conflicted. Often bad states of mind disappear when one makes an effort on behalf of the problem. Starting the term paper diminishes the anxiety over the looming deadline. Worry is not an action and not a solution. Action solves many problems.

States of mind that reveal suffering are an excellent diagnostic tool. They tell the listener where to look. That is, which narratives or missing actions are producing the suffering? A lot of pain in your stomach is a signal to see a doctor. A lot of anxiety over finances is a signal to take action about them. Suffering can be caused by inaction or conflicting, incompatible, or missing narratives.

States of mind at both extremes, positive and negative, cloud judgment. As I said before, observe your state of mind. It will distort your assumptions and could prejudice your actions. For example, a festive or ecstatic state of mind is not the right state of mind to be making investment decisions, nor is it a negative or panicked state of mind. It is vital to manage your state of mind when shifting narratives.

States of mind and music are connected. Music can reflect the spirit of the time. We can also use music to shift mindsets and evoke a story. Mozart produces a far different state of mind than Beethoven. Bob Dylan evokes a very different perspective than Motown. The Rolling Stones could not be confused with the Beatles. Frank Sinatra evokes a very different mood than Eminem.

EASY RIDER

There is something I haven't told you about leaving Cooke & Bieler for Silicon Valley. It is the other reason I made one of the most significant narrative shifts of my life. . It is one of the most potent lessons I've gained about state of mind shifts. It is the story of my brother David, who died at the age of thirty. I still miss him more than I usually admit.

David and the rest of the family called me "Zuz" growing up because I could not pronounce "Russell" as a small child. My brother was twenty-one months younger, which created a fair amount of sibling rivalry. The whole setup seemed unfair to me at times. There were certain privileges

I couldn't get until a certain age, like a later bedtime, but then as soon as I got them, he did too. He seemed to earn benefits by proxy rather than waiting.

But the accident that changed my life also changed everything between David and me. The rivalry disappeared, and he became very supportive, taking care of me and assisting me in any way he could. After that accident, we became very close. We double-dated went rock climbing and flew together in his airplane. In addition to flying planes, David also rode motorcycles, generally wore cowboy hats and boots, and enjoyed the West's wide-open spaces; he was a free spirit in every sense of the word.

David's narrative was that he would stay independent no matter what and always do his own thing. After a short stint in the Utah Air National Guard, he wanted to study aviation. He found that going to school interfered with his flying, so he dropped out and started a skydiving school instead.

David's love of flying extended beyond piloting small planes and parachuting out of them; he was also into BASE jumping, a type of advanced skydiving. BASE Jumping is an acronym standing for Building, Antennae, Span, and Earth, referring to the high places from which one can jump. BASE jumping has a person wearing a nylon-flying suit with fabric winglets under their arms that expand when they jump, essentially turning them into a flying squirrel. Daredevils like David jump from high-rise buildings and bridges, places where it's a straight drop to the ground. They get a running start, building to a sprint for the edge, and dive.

David had flown to California with some of his students to do an illegal jump off El Capitan, one of Yosemite's largest features. It was the early 80s, and he had just turned thirty. Jumping there was dangerous because of the uneven shape of the rock. He and his friends needed to get an even more massive running start to get the momentum they needed to clear the outward sloping cliff face. They wouldn't be able to open their chutes until they cleared the rocky cliff. One by one, David's students ran, leaped, and cleared El Capitan. Then it was his turn. Taking a deep breath, David went into a full sprint, arms pumping, the thick textured rubber soles of his jump boots slapping against the rock. He jumped.

David was too close to the wall, and his chute could not open all the way. This meant he could not steer and descended too quickly. Instead of landing in the drop zone, David fell with a loud, sickening thud onto some boulders in a nylon tangle of squirrel suit and parachute. David ended up breaking one leg very seriously. David was airlifted out.

David broke his leg so severely that it ended up being an inch shorter than his uninjured leg. For an independent, physical guy, always on the move, this was a defeating blow. For the time being, Easy Rider was sidelined. He began the long, arduous road of physical rehabilitation and threw himself into the task the best he could.

A couple of other things also happened during the year preceding David's death. One night, while driving home, David steered his car into a blind curve on the highway. A US Army Guard truck broken down on the side of the road hadn't set out flares, so David plowed right into it, creating a green metal mess. He wasn't hurt, but his car was totaled.

He loved that car, but he loved the girl he was living with at the time even more. It crushed David when he learned she was unfaithful. Betrayal was a turning point from which David was never able to recover. That same night he found out there was a fiery, emotional confrontation. David began drinking heavily and then added sleeping pills to the mix.

I was in Dallas at the time, on a research trip for Cooke & Bieler. At roughly five o'clock in the morning, the bedside phone rang. It was my classmate Robert who delivered the news. I could tell he was trying to be as gentle as possible.

July 19, 1981. David was dead of an accidental overdose.

My closest friend was dead. Despite David's known dark side, I can honestly say I did not see this coming, not in the least. David's unexpected death was, at the time, a bigger disaster than my blindness. I had time to adjust to my injuries, and the overwhelming feeling was of relief that I finally got to move forward. His loss came all at once, and I couldn't find a silver lining.

My brain worked overtime, mulling over the details, trying to make sense of it. David was finally turning a corner in recovering from his base-jumping accident and getting very fit. The word "accidental" seared itself into my brain. He was upset with his girlfriend, drank too much, and then added sleeping pills, and everything merged into a perfect storm, a tragedy. The coroner used the same word.

Accidental suicide.

Accidental was a legal distinction. How do you accidentally kill yourself? Suicide without intent?

When we are no longer able to change a situation, we are challenged to change ourselves.
—**Viktor E. Frankl**, *Man's Search for Meaning*

You can't control what happens to you, but you can control how you feel about it. You can control what you say about it to yourself and others. You can find meaning in adverse circumstances. You can choose your narrative to lead you out of those circumstances.

Accidental suicide.

The phrase "accidental" shifted my entire grieving process around David's death. The truth was that it was an accidental suicide. He had undertaken the actions that accidentally led to his death. Death was not some terrible, unexplainable phenomenon that "happened" to David, or even me, or our family. It was true that it happened, and now what would I say about it to myself? Was I going to be damaged, limited, and restrained in my life narrative because these bad things "happened" to me, first my accident and then David's? Or, was I going to take responsibility for both items, from the standpoint of being the owner of everything that happens to me? There was no one to be angry at, to lash out at; it was what it was. Others in my family kept a safe distance from their pain by stating, with forced certainty, that David's death was "God's plan." I was working from a different viewpoint, one of personal ownership.

After David's death, I felt pushed to answer some of life's deeper philosophical and spiritual questions. Ones that I'd never confronted before, even after my accident. I needed to go to a place that was conducive to such an exploration.

In Big Sur on the Northern California coast, the Esalen Institute, a spa with a hot water spring, has been around since the 1930s. Esalen was a magnet for some of the most famous philosophical and spiritual journeys. It was built for that purpose. It was a very permissive place with few rules beyond "don't hurt each other."

Esalen was what you wanted and needed it to be for you. I went to Esalen almost immediately after David's death.

I met Will Schutz, the Harvard professor and author, at Esalen. He taught me that life will be better once you assume that you cause everything that happens to you. It doesn't happen because you're a terrible person or that you're being tested or prepared for something bigger. Is the "God's plan" theory a shield to avoid confronting the universe's indifference and randomness? The realization that the universe is abundant and indifferent could create a very lonely existence. To think that life arose on Earth randomly is not the most comforting point of view. These are the types of life questions I grappled with while going on long hikes and soaking in the hot springs. I pondered the words now etched deeply in my mind "accidental suicide."

The word "accidental" understandably sent me backward in my narrative to my accident. I finally realized that I'd never reconciled that life-changing event. Instead, I became a laser-guided missile, locked on various targets based on my declarations. I focused only on getting the job at hand done. Suddenly, I was confronting not only my brother's death but also my close call with it. Was this by design, random, or something I caused? My lack of chemistry skill had undoubtedly caused the accident but was I also responsible for the severity of my injuries? In grieving my brother's death, I also began to grieve, for the very first time, the life that might have been for me.

A friend introduced me to the work of psychologist Elizabeth Kubler-Ross. She is well known for identifying grief stages: denial, anger, bargaining, depression, and acceptance. I realized that I was still in denial about what happened two decades after my accident. I had not dealt with my feelings about the accident. I read voraciously, searching every book for more answers and finding even more questions in the process. Jude Wanniski, the famous political economist, talks about the contingency of life and how "change only happens on the margin." In navigation, a small difference in heading leads to a big difference in the destination. The difference in the destination is more significant the longer the journey is. When we look back, it's easier to see how those changes that may have seemed minor at the time led us down a very different path than the one we were on. These are things we rarely realize at the time.

I realized that the answers I had to the questions I was now confronting were not good enough. My existing solutions were producing only misery and suffering. I even contemplated moving to Hong Kong just because it was a different part of the world. There were also parts of the world that I considered where someone could live inexpensively and disappear. But then I realized once I got there, I would still be me. I couldn't disappear from myself. "No matter where you go, there you are," as Buckaroo Banzai, channeling the Zen Masters, stated in the 1984 movie of the same name.

I felt suffocated at Cooke & Bieler, a racehorse in a traffic jam. David's death was a catalyst in my action to break free and head to Silicon Valley. I realized that more money would not produce more satisfaction or happiness. That hadn't worked so far; it just produced more money. David's passing created the spark that reminded me how important it is to live rather than merely exist in a moldy narrative. So, I shifted my story.

CHAPTER 10
DECLARATIONS

H ave you considered your suffering? Do you know whether it is due to inaction or an incomplete, faulty or missing narrative? You are now in a condition to make a declaration.

Declarations are the closest things we have to magic. They are the announcement of a new possibility and new action.

Declaration (n): A powerful statement describing a specific outcome, either desired or not desired, and always accompanied by action.

Why are declarations essential and necessary to create the life narrative that you want? Your very name was a declaration that someone made. When you develop principles that define what is forbidden, required, or allowed, you paint a picture of what is acceptable and what is not. A robust declaration can state conditions that you will and will not tolerate. It closes the possibilities that aren't consistent and always requires action. Here are three other things to consider when crafting a declaration:

1. **It needs to be public:** Statements of intention cannot exist in a vacuum. Public doesn't mean you have to put your declarations on Facebook. But it does mean you need to state it out loud, putting yourself on record for making the declaration. Making your statement public also puts you in a situation where people choose sides and support or oppose you. Creating polarization is an uncomfortable feeling. It is necessary to make the declaration real, versus a fleeting idea of something you may want but don't commit to. It's easy to say, "I'm declaring my support of world peace." Nobody will oppose that, and there is no specific action attached. That's not a declaration, it's an excellent and popular idea. A declaration is not a wish. Most of us confuse wishing and choosing. Many people wish for millions, for private jets, and better skills. Wishing, like hoping, is not an action. Choosing is an action. If you want two desirable but incompatible things, such as med school vs. law school, you must choose. Choice precedes declaration.

2. **It needs to be specific.** President Kennedy declared that the United States would put a man on the moon and bring him back alive before 1970. He defined a specific action. He specified a date certain.

3. **It needs to be supported and realized through actions with measurable results (metrics).** If you can't measure it, you can't manage it. Generating metrics is the best way to

observe actions and manage change. Metrics measure success or failure. Kennedy didn't say "someday." "Someday," there may be a second coming; that tells me nothing. He set a date, a measurable benchmark. Having metrics that measure outcomes is crucial. Useful measurements allow an outside observer to determine if the declaration is on course. It also allows you to choose if your declaration is on course.

DECLARING INDEPENDENCE

One of the most famous documents in history, and one of the two that founded America, begins with a declaration. I'm not referring to the Declaration of Independence, but the United States Constitution. The Constitution completely inverted the historical understanding of how power is granted. British colonists had brought a tradition of authority from the sovereign to the nobles, with only a small amount left over for the people. The modern English government was based on the Magna Carta under King John in 1215. The Magna Carta was a far more liberal arrangement than existed in any country at the time. The idea was to avoid a rebellion by the nobles. No one was concerned about a revolution by the people.

The U.S. Constitution inverted that hierarchy, creating law where power is held for and by the people. The Constitution grants authority from God, not a King. Our constitution is founded on the declaration that the government is the people's servant, not the master. The Constitution specifies **what is required, what is allowed, and what is forbidden.** The 9th and 10th amendments say that there is a list of Federal powers, and they are short. This is what "enumerated powers" means. If any powers are not on the list, you cannot later say, "Oh, they must have forgotten to add it." The Constitution's clarity is also why taxation of income, the prohibition of alcohol, and women voting required Constitutional amendments. These new powers and rights were outside of the original coverage area of what is required, what is allowed, and what is forbidden.

Our founding fathers put a lot of thought, specificity, and intention into the narrative of this new nation they were building. What is written down is more likely to be acted upon, and these men weren't taking any chances with their experiment's fate. The overall lesson here is that your declarations' specificity will lead to an increased chance of success in building a nation or shifting your life narrative. In America, the grant of power is from the people to the government, not the other way around. Power of the people was a new narrative about how power exists, who has it, and who can exercise it. This narrative shift explains a great deal, not only of America's historical greatness but about what declarations can do for you.

AVOIDING THE KOOL-AID

The people you surround yourself with will affect the declarations you make. Some will support your statements, but others will oppose you. When you make a declaration, be prepared to hear things like: "Well, that's silly. Don't you know that is impossible? I mean, how could that ever happen for you? That's a foolish thing for you to say." People take sides. People will either be with you or against you. People cannot be with you if they have decided what you are choosing to create in your life is impossible *for you*. Before making declarations be aware that people may try to drag you down. There's a real chance that you're going to finish this book all pumped up and enthusiastic, like a sprinter off the blocks. You may feel ready to take on the world with your newfound declarations, only to have someone in your life call you a fool. Are you strong enough to ignore those who doubt your declaration? Or is your declaration strong enough to keep you going no matter what?

It's not only the mortals who will stand in your way.

The universe will almost always oppose bold declarations. The more daring your declaration, the more powerful the obstacles the universe will throw in your path. The most important thing you can do is take immediate actions that are consistent with your declarations. For example, "I will not be dependent" translated to "go to school and get the skills needed to be independent." Because it's not that other person or people who are killing the declaration you've made. It's You. They don't have that power. But if their beliefs prevent you from taking action, then you have given them that power. It's not their words that can cause a declaration's failure, but rather your believing them. You either drink their Kool-Aid or say no thank you and take action as planned. Success is unusual enough without drinking the Kool-Aid of those who tell you your problems have nothing to do with you.

It is a dangerous narrative to believe that "I can't because I am blind/from a poor background/the wrong color," or whatever your limiting narrative is. Limiting narratives are excuses. Life is tricky, no matter who you are. Life doesn't particularly care about me more than it does the other guy. There's a Buddhist saying that **the universe is abundant but indifferent**. In Buddhist cosmology, the universe rewards that which is valuable.

The universe is not your life coach or your mother. Choices are yours to make. Shifting your narrative is not easy, but nothing is as bitter as being stuck with what you have declared to be unacceptable. However, there are abundant opportunities and possibilities if you take action. Significant change takes courage. Making your declaration and enduring opposition takes immense courage. I leave it up to you to choose whether you drink the Kool-aid and believe limiting narratives or whether you ignore your doubters and pursue your declaration. Besides not being a rocket scientist, I am also not a spiritual leader. I do, however, believe that the universe is abundant and indifferent.

DENIAL

It is vital to have strong declarations and never waver from them. I've often observed that people don't always see it this way. Sometimes, when obstacles occur between a person and their goal, it sets off a chain reaction of compromise and rationalization. They tell themselves and others, "Oh well, I didn't want that job anyway," and head off in a different direction. Rationalizing is an excellent way to end up somewhere other than where you wanted to go. Justifications are nothing but course alterations in disguise. They are tranquilizing narratives.

Tranquilizing narratives talk you into believing something is the right thing to do. The financial advisor who tells you to buy and hold and not worry may be selling you a tranquilizing narrative. Justifications can sound good, but they are Kool-Aid. "Those grapes were sour anyway." "I didn't want the job. I didn't want to be independent. Welfare is easier. A lot of good people are on welfare."

Accepting that the job doesn't matter and welfare is good enough euthanizes your prior declarations. Justification creates the real risk that months, years, or even decades later, you wake up in a life that seems normal. Don't forget that you chose not to be mediocre. Declarations are not enough. They need to be coupled with actions, especially when you falter. Failure is a learning opportunity, not proof that you cannot or should not continue to act. If you do not act in accordance with your declaration, you may end up somewhere you do not want to be. You lied to yourself. You deleted a declaration, and the course of your life changed. You went backward into the drift. Teddy Roosevelt said it best. *"It is not the critic who counts; not the man who points out how the strong man stumbles, or where the doer of deeds could have done them better. The credit belongs to the man who is actually in the arena, whose face is marred by dust and sweat and blood; who strives valiantly; who errs, who comes short again and again, because there is no effort without error and shortcoming; but who does actually strive to do the deeds; who knows great enthusiasms, the great devotions; who spends himself in a worthy cause; who at the best knows in the end the triumph of high achievement, and who at the worst, if he fails, at least fails while daring greatly, so that his place shall never be with those cold and timid souls who neither know victory nor defeat."*

PRESIDENTS

It was two years before the fall of the Soviet Union, and I was about to meet the President, the elder Bush, George H.W.

Bush wasn't the first president I'd shaken hands with. Back in the early 80s, Uncle Jake arranged a meeting with President Reagan. The Bush meeting, however, was based on my merit. Senator Bob Dole had just appointed me to the United States Commission on Civil Rights. There was a ceremony in the Rose Garden where Bush announced my appointment to the press. Then my guide dog and I were escorted by the Secret Service into the Oval Office.

I found President Bush to be much more impressive in person than on TV. He was much taller than I thought.

You may be wondering how a blind person would know how tall someone is or anything else about him or her. Over the years, I've developed a new ability to be an observer. Observation of this kind isn't based on eyesight or even hearing. Those are physical senses. One's capacity for being an observer, almost like a new dimension, is based on distinctions like what they can "listen" for rather than simply hear. I can tell a lot about a person's size, age, weight, and mood in a short conversation. I can also make pretty accurate assessments about them like personality, character, etc.

When I met President Bush, the first thing he did was kneel to shake my dog's paw. The White House photographer captured the moment.

Mother saw the photo, got very excited, and exclaimed in a moment of maternal hyperbole, "Russell, I always *knew* that presidents would kneel to you!"

CHAPTER 11
ACTIONS

The rooster thinks that his crowing causes the sun to rise. The Native Americans believed that rain dances cause rain to happen. Actions without understanding hold little weight.

—Russell Redenbaugh

Landing Metal Birds

During World War II, some South Pacific islands were staging areas for American military inventory. Hulking silver metal cargo planes would land. Soldiers would rush out and unload all cargo types in giant boxes. They delivered food, batteries, weapons, survival gear, housing, equipment, and more. The plane would then take off to refill with more cargo. The process repeated this way throughout the war. As it turns out, those cargo planes and soldiers were being watched and carefully.

The South Pacific island natives peered down at the runways from hilltops. From their hiding spots behind bushes and trees, they spied in fascination at the big metal birds. Where did these birds come from, they wondered? Why were they always full of food and survival supplies? The islanders had no understanding of an airplane, so they concluded that the big metal birds came from the heavens.

Further, they noted the exact procedures required to call forth the birds from the sky. They memorized the sequence of events that needed to happen to bless the people on the ground with food and supplies. The islanders thought they were witnessing a real miracle, and they began to worship the big metal birds. The tribal elders decided that everyone should learn the steps to please the gods. The gods that sent these planes and the precious life-giving cargo inside. Anthropologists would later name this belief system the Cargo Cult.

In the meantime, the islanders benefited from those Army Air Corps bases during WWII. The military created jobs for the natives, resulting in much better food and conditions on the islands. Their conditions improved from their former lives as hunters, gatherers, farmers, and fishers. They no longer had to survive on fish, coconuts, yams, and whatever else they could hunt or grow.

When the war ended and the military cleared out, they left quite a bit of cargo. This included the air traffic control tower and runway where the giant metal birds once landed. The islanders were not worried. They had studied for years all the physical actions needed to make the metal birds and their cargo arrive from the heavens. They sat in the tower, in their tribal clothes, wearing aviation headsets made of coconuts and speaking into palm frond microphones. They chanted prayers to the gods to make the metal birds come back. Some of them ran up and down the runway, waving their arms the way the soldiers had as they were landing the planes. Still others stood off to the side of the runway, peering into the sky, waiting to unload the cargo once the birds landed. The birds never came, and the islanders blamed themselves and vowed to the gods that they would try harder. Their ritual's failure was their only explanation for why the metal birds were not coming—they must not be working hard enough. But of course, the birds never came. Anthropologists later found this scene when they stumbled upon these cargo cults after World War II.

The islanders' declaration was: we will call forth the metal birds and all their cargo to supply our island. They did not understand how airplanes were used. They did not have a rudimentary understanding of aviation. The narrative they created mimicked the military's narrative. The natives then mimicked the soldiers' actions to bring that narrative to life. When it didn't work, they continued to emulate, but with more intensity. They worked around the clock in shifts, desperately trying to please the gods so they would send down the metal birds.

The cargo cults came from a powerful narrative of the natives themselves. "The indigenous societies of Melanesia were a "big man" political system. In such a system, individuals gained prestige through gift exchanges. The more wealth a man could distribute, the more people in his debt, and the greater his renown. The Melanesians called those who were unable to reciprocate "Rubbish Men." The Melanesians encountered people with seemingly unlimited resources. They ended up being dominated by their narrative and feeling like "Rubbish Men." It is easy to judge and laugh at an unfamiliar culture, but we fall prey to the same narrative fallacies ourselves. Imitating others does not work. "If I do every single thing that Tony Robbins has done in his life to be successful, make the same decisions he has, make the same stock investments, dress the way he dresses, and act the way he acts, I will be as successful as him," we think.

Like the cargo cults trying to replicate the results achieved by technology that they do not understand, the Tony Robbins Impersonator is only touching the surface of what makes Tony Robbins such a huge success. The clear alternative to this is to rewrite your narrative, not imitate others on a surface level.

Mimicking without full understanding will never produce the same results. Such aping reminds me of some of the tips-and-tricks-thinking that is so prevalent. "Do these ten things, and your life will change." As far as I know, that only worked once, and it involved Moses with a stone tablet on a mountaintop.

Tips, steps, and other paint-by-number ways of thinking do a disservice in that they hide the complicated way the world works. There is no easy way to change, but there is a simple and profound way. There are no "10 easy steps" to change the world or even your world.

Leslie, my friend, and student learned this while attending one of my Miraval Spa investment seminars. She said that I taught her how to "see" and found the irony of learning to see from a blind person delicious.

Leslie Bruhn, a successful CPA on the California central coast, told me, "I remember the world opening up for me as you spoke. But then I looked around the room and saw, to my surprise, that nobody else seemed to be experiencing the same lightning bolts. At first, I thought I was reading too much into your lessons, and maybe I was crazy. And it hit me! They didn't have the same experience that I was having because they had come to the seminar looking for quick tips and simple formulas that they could take home and use to get rich overnight. They didn't get that you were teaching them how to see—how to observe—and then shift their entire money narrative as a result." This book and my methods are for people who value hard work and results over quick fixes.

In one of the greatest and most moving speeches of all time, Winston Churchill made a powerful declaration. That declaration led to the defeat of the fearsome German war machine. In the same speech, he spelled out that things worth achieving are rarely easy. *"I have nothing to offer but blood, toil, tears, and sweat. We have before us an ordeal of the most grievous kind. We have before us many, many long months of struggle and of suffering. You ask, what is our policy? I will say: It is to wage war, by sea, land, and air, with all our might and with all the strength that God can give us; to wage war against a monstrous tyranny, never surpassed in the dark and lamentable catalog of human crime. That is our policy. You ask, what is our aim? I can answer in one word: victory. Victory at all costs, victory in spite of all terror, victory, however long and hard the road may be; for without victory, there is no survival."*

Kennedy made a similar point outside of hot wartime in that speech that would so affect my destiny in 1962 *"...We choose to go to the Moon in this decade... not because [it is] easy, but because [it is] hard; because that goal will serve to organize and measure the best of our energies and skills, because that challenge is one that we are willing to accept, one we are unwilling to postpone, and one we intend to win."*

Mimicking may appear to work to a certain degree. In investing, if you read all the tips and tricks, do what others do, and follow directions, you are only imitating actions, not understanding them. The danger is that you may appear to succeed. But if you want to be excellent and get the best results, you must gain a much deeper understanding of what is occurring and then innovate. Full understanding may take a lifetime, but the only test of knowledge is doing. Long-term, market-beating performance is unlikely to occur in the absence of focused attention and old-fashioned hard work. Things worth doing are rarely easy.

EFFECTIVE ACTION

You've located a limiting narrative and taken the crucial action of making a bold declaration. But the job of shifting your story is not complete. Continue to take practical steps that move you toward fulfilling your declaration. Move away from what you will not tolerate and toward that which you have announced you will have more of.

Action and motion are not the same. The cargo cult followers were making motions, but they were not taking effective action. In the same way, movement and motivation are not the same.

Motivation only lasts when coupled with a new set of actions. Shifting your narrative is not about being motivated for a moment but rather about taking action permanently through new habits and behaviors.

Similarly, action and activity are not the same. For example, imagine you are at Deer Valley Ski Resort and see someone skiing in the distance. The movement they are doing is skiing. But what is their real action? Action requires an interpretation of the circumstances and setting. The skier may be working on ski patrol, skiing for fun, or training for the winter Olympics.

Louisa Gilder is the daughter of George Gilder. George is an influential thinker on technology, information theory, and economics. He is my longtime friend and mentor. George has written nineteen books, many of which are worldwide bestsellers. Several years back, Louisa made the declaration that she would write a book on quantum physics. Louisa wanted to write the book, had all the knowledge and information at her disposal to do the job, and knew that this was the perfect time to get it done. However, Louisa suddenly stalled a bit because she didn't have the ideal setting to take more effective actions. She realized that her family home was too active a place for a first-time writer. Her father, George, encouraged Louisa to come out to California to stay with me. Louisa was a brilliant, confident young woman who didn't have any self-limiting narratives. She did not tell herself, "I'm not good enough," "I can't do this," or "Girls can't do the math." She graduated from Dartmouth with a 4.0 GPA. She was on Dartmouth's ski team, a disciplined elite athlete. She needed support in the action piece, and we were happy to help.

Fortunately, Louisa knew she needed support and structure and drove out West. Sure enough, once she stayed in our guest bedroom, Louisa got the focus she needed to take action and complete her book. Much of the support we provided was the constant encouragement, "Go to your room and don't come back until you've written 1,000 words."

Louisa finished *The Age of Entanglement: When Quantum Physics Was Reborn*. Critics received it well. She is currently working on her second book, but not in our guest room this time.

The lesson about action from Louisa's story is that you need to take several other steps to achieve a declaration after making one. For Louisa, she needed to remove herself from family, friends, and college distractions. Louisa made a declaration, and we provided a physical space where she could work without distraction. We also provided guidance and structure for her work.

The reason that action is by far the most challenging piece of the Shift model is that it is human beings' nature to procrastinate. It is also easy for us to remain asleep in the drift, unconscious to our procrastination. For example, many tell themselves, "I'll start saving for retirement next year" until too many years have passed.

We can create the most specific, determined declarations in the world and then shape them with powerful narratives, but it's all talk and pipe dreams without effective action. This is why deadlines exist in publishing. Editors enforce those deadlines, essentially telling writers, "go to your room and don't come back until you've written your 1,000 words."

Our propensity for procrastination is also why we have managers, bosses, and for some, coaches, mentors, and consultants. They hold us accountable for completion and help keep us on course. In my experience, being held liable to action and getting guidance from an outside party creates the best results.

THE DISCIPLINE TO NOT DO WHAT YOU WANT

There's nothing more useless than a runway that's behind you or an altitude that's above you.

—Russell Redenbaugh

Successful people are excellent at closing possibilities. That's the nature of choice—when you choose one option, you eliminate others. I have a friend named Rusty Holden. I first met him on an airplane and concluded on the spot that he was completely crazy, but in a good way. He is a real-life mad scientist who had developed many different nuclear power plans for plants and atomic isotopes. He had commercialized none of them. Rusty didn't have a problem with ideas; he had a problem with completion. He didn't want to give up on anything that might become something. And when you have that many potential "somethings," how can you tell which is the winning idea?

I knew that if he didn't pick one idea and commercialize it, he would remain a brilliant but needy mad scientist. I started to help Rusty close other attractive possibilities to pursue just one by asking a series of simple but leading questions.

"Are you married, Rusty?"

"Well, yes."

"Happily?" I asked.

"Yes," he answered.

"Well, when you got married, you closed other possibilities, didn't you? Are you sorry you did that?" I asked.

"Well, no," he said.

"Good," I said, "Now which one of these good ideas will you marry?"

Next, I flipped the conversation into one of scientific reasoning. Sometimes the best-received advice is spoken in the recipient's language.

"Start with the end in mind," I told Rusty.

"What do you mean by that?" he said.

"Which invention is most likely to produce a short-term liquidity event?" I asked, referring to the end goal of commercializing the invention and creating a profitable company.

"Hmmm," he said. "Medical, because nuclear power plants are impossible to build in the U.S."

"Good. Let's take all the nuclear power plant projects off the table. Now, which of your medical inventions is most likely to find a market wherein somebody would buy your company, or more importantly, invest in it once you do a proof of concept?"

Rusty picked one invention to commercialize. The mad scientist was overwhelmed by opportunity, but by removing all but one possibility, he could take practical action.

Rusty reminded me that brilliance is not enough. What the universe rewards is the person who sticks with a single idea and pursues it relentlessly. It's not just about being smart. If it were, the world would be crawling with many more legendary success stories in every discipline. As I told Rusty, "Focus, focus, focus. Do one thing, do one thing again, and then do it more." As tempting as it is to want to do everything, the discipline to avoid that temptation is the difference between finishing something successfully and being overwhelmed.

The state of overwhelm is the inability to close possibilities. Overwhelm results in a lousy mood and inaction, which some people call procrastination. Bad attitudes show up when you're not in purposeful action. It all starts with closing possibilities. Like how there is a meager return on investment being the victim, there is also an extremely low ROI on being unwilling to choose one option and act. Both, by the way, are declarations. You are either making the declaration that you will make a choice or making the declaration that you will not choose. Not choosing is a choice.

It is human nature to procrastinate and say "yes" until we are finally overcommitted.

For instance, we have a terrible habit of asking our staff to do more than they can realistically get done. This is our weakness, but we let new employees know this when we hire them. We tell them, "Now we will ask, and ask, and ask, but it's up to you to have the skill to say, 'Well sure Russell, I'll do that, but that means I won't be able to do this other thing.'" We let new employees know that they won't be very successful working for us if they can't learn this. Good employees learn how to say, "No." The bad employees wander off.

Asking employees to make hard decisions may seem unkind, but if you think about it, you are faced with this situation every day. The only difference is, you're not being told about it outright. Your boss, the PTA at your child's school, and your friends are not collectively saying, "Now, we're going to try and pile so many requests and responsibilities on you that if you don't say no to some of them, you will crack." It's your job to say no. If you can't successfully say no, overwhelm happens.

TIME TO ACT

Taking effective action isn't easy, but that's not because it is intrinsically difficult. Instead, most of us simply don't know how to do it. Here are some of the distinctions and steps I have successfully used to change my life.

Promises

Promises are the way we interact successfully with others. Would you rely on someone, a friend, or a business, which repeatedly failed to keep its promises? No. In America, we live in deep cultural confusion about what a commitment is. Some of us honestly believe we have not made a promise if we don't say the words, "I promise." This breakdown causes mistrust and suspicion. A powerful way to separate yourself from the uncoordinated masses and become effective is to implement two "promise strategies." 1) Listen for promises in all conversations. 2) Be aware of making promises in all exchanges.

A promise exists when four conditions are present. The first two conditions are that the listener and the speaker each understands what a commitment is. For example, a toddler cannot understand nor make a promise. A sixteen-year-old may understand what a contract is, but we should seriously doubt their capacity to carry out large and long-term commitments.

The third element of a promise is Conditions of Satisfaction, or the "what" the promisor has agreed to provide. The more each party understands the Conditions of Satisfaction, the better. For example, around the house, a man may promise his wife to do all the shopping for the family's July 4th picnic. She accepts, and when he arrives home with three-dozen hot dogs, buns, chips, and two cases of beer, his wife's unhappiness surprises him. There was no meeting of the minds about what a shopping list for the picnic meant. Effective communication would have been more specific about what is on and not on the shopping list. The husband went shopping for the party, but he did not fulfill the promise understood by his wife.

Another example frequently occurs in business, specifically meetings. A CEO calls his top executives to a critical strategy session. The CFO, COO, Head of Sales, and Director of Marketing all prepare extensively, producing in-depth examinations into their departments. But when they arrive, the CEO reads his plan to discuss high-level, outside-of-the-box ideas about the company's strategy in ten years. Since each team member assumed that "strategy session" meant reviewing their respective roles, none of them have prepared. All that they discuss is scheduling the next meeting. Effective communication from the CEO would have specified the condition of satisfaction for a "strategy brainstorming" meeting.

The fourth element of a promise is the time when the promise will be fulfilled. This is also called "date certain," to use the even more exact language of finance. *"A date certain is the exact date by which a specified action must occur, according to a particular contract. The date certain is an important piece of information because it is legally binding on the parties involved."* *Investopedia.* We all know about deadlines: taxes due, school paper due, license renewal due. Time is often precise and imposed by outside forces. But the time that destroys effective action is time that is not imposed by an outsider like the DMV or IRS. It's time we self-impose like, "I'll do it later" or "I'll do it at the end of next week." For a promise to be rigorous, time must be either specified or clearly understood. For example, a manager who promises to "deliver the report by the end of the week" sets himself up for an unsatisfied boss. Although this would not get him fired in America, it doesn't increase his value in the least. A more valuable manager makes a promise that "The report will be on your desk by 4 p.m. Thursday, does that work for you?"

For my partner at Kairos Capital Advisors, James Juliano, the learning began before he even started on the job. On the day that I made him an employment offer, and he promised to accept or reject my offer by a specific date. As a fresh university graduate and busy Wall Street rookie, James did not have the same refined understanding about promises as I did. James accepted my offer after alerting his investment-banking employer about his notice to leave and take a new job. However, he accepted 8 hours past the promised deadline.

My response was, "I am happy to hear your decision, but my offer is withdrawn."

James learned the importance of promises. Chastened and jobless, James offered to come work for free as an "economic research volunteer" until he'd proven his value. We let him do that but only let him suffer without pay for a very short time. To this day, James, now my business partner, friend, and most trusted advisor, has never lost sight of the importance of promises. Of course, the word "promise" was never said, but we exchanged promises with the job offer.

A promise is a commitment between two people who understand what a promise is. Promises are powerful and allow us to coordinate our actions with others. They make the world work. When you listen and speak rigorously regarding promises, you're ready for the next step.

Requests and Offers

We are request machines. We live our lives making requests. Unfortunately, most requests are sloppy. For example, in long-term relationships, it's common to say, "I'm tired," or "I'm hungry," or "I'm bored." Yet, in the context of the relationship, these are requests masquerading as announcements. The way to make a more rigorous request is to apply the conditions of a promise. Replace "I'm hungry" with "could you please make dinner within the next hour." Ensure both parties understand it is a request, with sufficient conditions of satisfaction and a time certain for completion.

An offer is a conditional promise. Like a request, a rigorous offer must meet the requirement of a promise, like conditions of satisfaction and time of completion. For example, "I offer to paint your kitchen for $500 next Tuesday." Offers are far more potent than requests because they create value if your offer delivers something the receiver wants.

Let's pull these distinctions together into an example of useful actions. A wife and mother of two makes a declaration to her family, "I will learn to play the cello well enough to play in our community orchestra in less than one year." She follows up on that declaration by taking the following actions:

She makes promises to her husband, like, "I won't spend more than five hours per week learning to play the cello. I will organize my lessons and practice times so that they do not interfere with after-school homework and family mealtimes."

She makes requests, like finding a local cello instructor and requesting to be a student. She clarifies what she will learn, what times the lessons are, and how much she will pay.

She makes offers, like helping the cello instructor with his business's paperwork in exchange for sitting in on lessons with other students.

Through effective actions like these, she is on her way to fulfilling her declaration.

DESIGNING FOR ACTION

Here are some useful rules that will help keep your declarations and supporting actions coherent to increase your chances of affecting change.

Mentorship

Mentorship is a powerful tool in shifting narratives because mentors have the advantage of seeing the big picture. Mentors have different perspectives on a topic or situation to which the mentee is blind.

Case in point, one of our employees who helped us with tasks around the house was working on her MBA. She told me how overwhelmed she was by the complexities of the financial lessons, particularly accounting. I decided to spend some time with her to help change her narrative.

"You know," I told her one day over lunch, "finance is not complicated. Someone who has not yet taken her first accounting course may find finance mystifying. However, someone who has completed an introductory course will find it simple since debits and credits are always equal. Complication is an assessment made by an observer; it is not the truth.

In other words, something becomes complicated when you look at it from the point of view that doesn't see the fundamentals of what is happening. By having a narrative that learning accounting was hard, the employee had created a climate of stress and resistance around her learning. I helped shift her understanding by showing her different perspectives of her "finance is hard" narrative, which she hadn't previously seen.

The student can only look from where they look. You can't tell someone to "look from a different perspective" because they don't know what that means. "See it differently" is not an operational instruction. Instead, and as I did with this young woman, the mentor's message should be: "There are people who understand this phenomenon. From where you are as a beginner, you simply cannot see the big picture that I see." And from there, you bring them step-by-step into the picture, widening the lens with each principle and lesson.

I showed her that finance was no different than a more complicated checkbook.

Mentoring is never a one-way street. For me, the best way to learn something is to teach it to someone who has no idea what you're talking about. If you can understand a topic well enough to explain it to a beginner, then you have mastered the subject. "If you can't explain it simply, you don't understand it well enough" – Albert Einstien Mentoring means being able to remove complexity and boil a topic down to the essence. A good teacher or mentor can help the student learn a topic in a simple way. If you understand your subject, you can explain it simply to people who have no background in it. The only reason that I am at all "qualified" to take on the role of mentor in this book is that I've been studying what it takes to shift narratives for most of my life. I lived within the Shift model, and I can make it accessible for you and others.

I met Bill Coleman in 2000 in Salt Lake City while I was looking into buying a bankrupted 3,500-acre ranch. The plan was to convert it into five to twenty-acre residential horse properties. Bill connected me with the people I needed to know to make the project happen, and in return (as I have the habit of doing), I shared my Shift model. One of our first conversations took place as we drove down a long two-lane highway to look at the ranch property.

"What do you care about in life?" I asked him at one point.

Bill rambled on about family, feel-good things, work, the housing industry, current events, and other items central to his world.

"Well, you know that each of the things you listed is something you care about, but how passionate are you really about any of the things you just listed? How rich and meaningful are they to you, especially with regard to where you want your life to go?"

He soon realized that none of his present declarations prompted strong enough answers. From there, he built a narrative based on discovering how he could have a more significant impact on his world. In other words, he asked the right questions to find out what others cared about and then performed the actions to deliver to them. Questioning has, in turn, added a new level of depth and intensity to Bill's world.

"What I've done is pay it forward too, the Shift model," Bill told me recently while we were fly fishing in Park City, Utah. "Finding out so much about my narrative has changed my life, and it's been exciting to pass it on."

The impromptu role of mentor that I took on with Bill is not unusual for me. Perhaps because of the things I've gone through, probably because I'm a teacher by nature or a combination of the two, this tends to happen with many people I encounter. Reading between the lines, hearing the things they're not saying, I identify a way to help them change their declarations, create new actions, and shift their narrative. As a mentor for life, I can't help myself; there's no "off" switch.

The challenge is finding enough good mentees to receive this knowledge. Yes, that's right, there is a shortage of good mentees for mentors who wish to guide them. Mentors don't suffer fools gladly. Thus, if you are an excellent mentee, you can always find the best mentors. You are the scarce resource, not them.

So, what makes a good mentee? Surrender. A good mentee can suspend suspicion, mistrust, and hostility and receive the information. Trust doesn't mean that they turn their brains off and drink the Kool-Aid. But it does mean the temporary suspension of disbelief. They replace "Well, that can't be right!" with more of a curiosity, "That's so different from what I've learned. Tell me why you say that." Curiosity versus cynicism. A good mentee is also fascinated by a deep understanding of the topic at hand versus collecting "tips and techniques" to tide them over.

There is a similar distinction between mentors and teachers. Mentoring is not about transferring knowledge but skills. Knowing is only proven by doing, and a mentor builds that capacity for action within the mentee.

A good mentor also holds a vision for the mentee of what the mentee can become, especially when the mentee can't envision their future. The mentor also helps when the mentee is overwhelmed by what they don't know. The mentor helps them along in the narrative, manages their mood, and reinforces that knowledge is only useful when attached to a capacity for action. A mentor helps describe a possible future (assuming the mentee does his or her part of following the lessons and taking the correct steps).

Mentees must measure *relative* progress. Measuring their progress does not mean comparing the mentee's progress against the mentor's much more significant life experience.

The lesson here for mentors is not to produce a negative assessment of the mentee based on a very unfair mentor/mentee comparison. The mentees' task is to avoid standing against a yardstick so tall that they can never possibly measure up.

Dr. Fernando Flores is a philosopher, entrepreneur, and Chilean politician. I met him during the 1980s in Silicon Valley. Seeing the value of his knowledge and experience, I attached myself to him and ran one of his companies. I always felt that the most value I received from Dr. Flores was his knowledge, more so than the paychecks he wrote for me.

A successful mentoring relationship is mutually beneficial. Each party, mentor, and mentee must be satisfied that they receive value; the scales have to balance.

Some people I've seen have a somewhat distorted view of what a mentor should offer them. They see a mentor as an unlimited Rolodex of contacts, connections, and opportunities. An uneven relationship is by no means mutually beneficial—a mentor connecting a mentee with his network in exchange for what? Besides, the mentor is taking on an enormous risk, putting his reputation on the line. Imagine if he connects the mentee with his network, and the mentee fails or misbehaves. It would be complicated for the mentor to rebuild that trust and rapport with his network. Relationships are more valuable than money. You can always make your money back, but not your reputation.

Overall, mentoring is a much more intimate and more trust-based relationship than coaching or guidance. Throughout the book, you've met some of the people whom I've mentored along the way. They are all recipients of the Shift message that I came up with years ago, and most were willing recipients. You've also met some of my mentors, like Art Laffer, George Gilder, and Dr. Flores.

As I've moved through these relationships and others, I've learned that a mentor must be willing—and even eager—to see his or her mentee outgrow them. A dedicated mentor celebrates this, rather than letting ego get in the way and feeling discarded or useless. All too many times, I've seen poor mentors form a needy relationship with their mentees. They stifle mentees from growing too far and expanding beyond them.

Some parents do this as well, which is unfortunate since a good parent's job is to render themselves obsolete.

Mini Max

Phil Migliarese is a 5th degree Brazilian Jiu-jitsu black belt with an impressive track record as both competitor and trainer. He owns Balance Studios in Philadelphia with his brother Ricardo.

We finished a lesson one day, and Phil shared how he thought about opening his first gym.

"Well, couldn't that be financially risky?" I asked him.

"Yes," he said, "but there isn't any other way to do it, is there?"

I told him, "Actually, there are two strategies you can pursue, and both relate to the fighting strategies I've seen you use in tournaments. You've never used the maxi-max strategy, meaning maximize your maximum return. You never do the flashy thing that could work spectacularly, but if you don't do it perfectly, you could lose it all."

"That's true," Phil agreed.

"You do mini-max instead, meaning minimize your maximum regret. In fighting, your maximum regret is a loss, not a less flashy win. So, your fight strategy is the tortoise rather than the hare. You win in little increments. You let the other person have your way. So, what are the ways you do this in opening a business? How could you still start your gym while minimizing your maximum loss?"

Bingo. Light bulb on! Phil got what I was saying when I connected a new business challenge with something familiar to him, his fighting style. Phil now calls what I taught him "business Jiu-jitsu."

You probably already use mini-max strategies. They include carrying life, health, car, and excess liability insurance. You prepare for a bad outcome and hope it doesn't happen. Now that you see this as minimizing your maximum regret review your coverages to make sure they are high enough.

Mini-max is one of the strategies I use for designing everything I do. Most people go through life with hopes and expectations that they do not derive from evidence. Minimizing your maximum regret recognizes that not all plans stay on the "happy path," and bad things do happen.

STRUCTURE OF INCENTIVES

An incentive is a payment or benefit that may cause a behavioral change. Children learn about incentives early. Eat your peas, and you'll get dessert. Remember the job jar with chores and payments for completion written on pieces of paper? From this simple beginning, incentives become an increasing part of our "structures" as we mature.

The structure of incentives shapes our behaviors. We all tend to act consistently with incentives because we understand them. Some incentives are so clear and powerful that the action is easy. The consequence of not paying the IRS is going to jail, and most of us pay our taxes without protest because of the negative incentive.

Beyond this obvious example, the incentives structure is often confused or lost when designing our actions. Ignoring incentives for yourself and others will have a bad outcome.

Residential real estate sales commission is typically six percent of the sales price. You may naively think your incentives and the selling agent's are aligned; the higher the selling price, the higher the agent's commission. But wait, this is wrong, as proven by Steven Levitt in his 2005 bestseller *Freakonomics: A Rogue Economist Explores the Hidden Side of Everything*. The real deal is that the agent maximizes their income from a quick sale, and a quick sale is most often realized from a lower price. To secure a higher price requires a longer time on the market and additional marketing expense paid by the agent. To test his hypothesis, Levitt compared the length of time that agent-owned houses were on the market versus their clients' homes. Agents behavior was different when selling their own homes than when selling other people's homes because the structure of incentives is different.

What is the structure of incentives for elite universities' admissions committees? The title "admission committee" leads you to believe their job is to admit the best students. It is not. From the viewpoint of the student, the admissions committee's job is not to accept you. It is to find reasons why your application belongs in the discard pile. Those reasons to not admit line up with each school's structure of incentives. Do they want a well-balanced student body or a higher-than-average number of "eccentrics"? Knowing the committees' system of incentives influences where and how prospects apply to schools.

What is the structure of incentives for traditional financial advisors? The nice man helping you select the correct mutual fund for your retirement will receive compensation based on the products he sells you. There is a conflict of interest when he sells you an investment product to earn commission while telling you that product is in your best interest. It may be in your best interest, but the structure of incentives forces commission-based advisors to frequently make poor choices for the client.

Always stop and ask the question "Who benefits?" as the German philosopher Hegel taught. James and I use this question in our investment advisory businesses when making political and economic assessments: "Follow the money." People will generally act out of their self-interest and rarely yours. We invest our own and our clients' money following our narrative of "Policy-Based Investing." Government economic policies set the rules of the game and alter the structure of incentives for companies, sectors, and entire countries. When government policies change, the system of incentives change, and we identify when and where those changes happen.

Think about our experience with technology rapidly changing the entire structure of incentives. As George Gilder wrote in *Microcosm* in

1989, "The transformation from moving atoms to bits at light speed will topple the structures of power." We have seen the elimination of entire industries based on technology changing the structure of incentives. The music and book industries are two of the best examples. No one sent a memo that brick-and-mortar music and bookstores would so rapidly disappear, but the structure of incentives caused their customers to flee.

Following the structure of incentives works at the country level as well; how could it not? French President Hollande decided to increase taxes on France's wealthiest residents in 2012. Since France, like most countries, taxes on residency, not citizenship, the tax rate hike shifted an essential piece of incentives' structure. When tax rates skyrocketed, wealthy French residents interpreted the law as a request to move to Belgium, where French is also spoken.

The above examples demonstrate that the structure of incentives explains behaviors. Well-designed actions must acknowledge this

CONCLUSION
STYLE, STRUCTURE, AND SUMMARY

We humans are unique creatures; we can do nearly anything we want. As my dad always said in an early economics lesson, "You can have anything you can pay for."

I have had many victories, many failures, some significant accomplishments, and some disappointments. But I did what I have done, had a great life, and it is not over yet. The best may be yet to come. Who knows? I've already done much more than I ever thought possible since those fifty-plus years ago when a homemade rocket explosion changed my life forever.

But despite all that I have accomplished, I often think that I could have done so much more. For instance, I should have written this book sooner.

When I set out to write this book, I thought it would be much more complicated than it turned out to be. I also believe that I've produced a better volume than I anticipated when I began. Surprising simplicity is not a reflection of the value of my story or the Shift model. This reluctance on my part was purely about the question I kept asking myself whenever the subject of writing a book came up: Who cares?

For years, I found the idea of writing a book about myself a bit self-indulgent and narcissistic. I had the same objection when the producers asked me to do the Tedx Talk about my life. Even after the talk, as I left the stage, I still didn't fully understand the point of telling my story. I have come to know that the real message is, "If I can do it, so can you." The goal was to turn my life story and knowledge I've picked up along the way into an actionable model that people can follow to shift their narratives and live a better life. Once I finally realized the difference between telling a story and offering an actionable model for a genuine shift, the whole process began. Perhaps I should have written this book sooner.

CLOSING THOUGHTS

We all live in narratives. We have ideas about who we are, what happens to us, and why our situation is as it is. We form stories about the careers we choose, the friends we have, and the places we go. These self-generated stories both expand and limit our opportunities. Most of us believe our circumstances produce our narratives. But what if our narratives produce our circumstances?

Whether you believe it or not, you already possess the capability to have more of what you care about. Your narratives blind you. A different narrative produces a different you. It's not easy, nor is it an instantaneous change. But you can do it. There are tools you can use now to start having more of what you care about. You can't win a gold medal in Jiu-jitsu tomorrow, but you can begin shifting your narrative to make that a possibility today.

EPILOGUE
BACK ON THE MAT

September 2015

N ow finish him!" my coach bellowed, screaming above the crowd noise.

Grappling with my opponent, Alexandre "Xande" Ribeiro, a 210-pound, seven-time world champion black belt, all I can think is, "Am I doing this at seventy years-old?"

It's the International BJJ Master Senior Jiu-jitsu Tournament and takes place once a year. It used to be in Rio de Janeiro, the same location where I experienced my initial victories. Now it's in Las Vegas, where it draws a dramatically larger attendance; they sold every ticket weeks before the registration deadline. There are also more contestants, 3,000 this year and far more than the organizers planned over two days. They ran fourteen simultaneous matches.

But I would not be a contestant in this event. I stopped entering tournaments in 2005 after winning my third world championship. I figured I'd quit while I was ahead, and now I'm a decade beyond the upper age limit. They did ask me back to perform a few different demonstrations, though. The demonstration was my way of thanking the BJJ organization and the sport of Jiu-jitsu for all it had done to improve my life.

I flew to Las Vegas with my trainer, Eduardo, days before the event to get ready. I hadn't trained in nearly five weeks, and did I mention I was now seventy years old? Not that age matters; that's a narrative I discarded long ago when I got into Jiu-jitsu at age fifty. For example, at the gym, I routinely tap out black belts in their thirties. But they aren't world champs, I am. They're young and healthy, but I know a different set of moves. The other guys at my gym have caught on, but I catch a new guy from time to time. During my training in Las Vegas before the demonstration, I tapped out three black belts. None of these three had seen any of these submissions before now.

"What was THAT?" an opponent exclaimed during one of our practice sessions.

"That was a foot lock," I replied calmly.

"Yeah, but you didn't use your hands!!"

"Yes, it's a foot lock done with my feet," I answered him.

"Yes, but your foot locked my foot," he persisted.

"That's why it's called a foot lock," I said.

It's not an age narrative. It's an experience narrative.

Before my match with the 210-pound, seven-time champion, they announced that this would be my last fight. I was retiring from competition but continuing to train twice a week. I received a nice ovation from the crowd, who looked at my monster-sized opponent and figured out that it was a demonstration and not a real match. Barring any severe mistakes by Goliath, there's no way I could have defeated him in an open competition.

First, he toyed with me, letting me demonstrate some moves for the crowd, like escapes from his guard and takedowns. It was a five-minute match, so that took up about four minutes.

With one minute to go, Eduardo yelled to finish him. That was the clue for him not to defend quite so hard and for me to attack. I turned on all the energy I'd been saving and put what's called a knee in the belly. Then I went for a choke, which was pointless since I couldn't come close to getting my good hand around his monster neck, and he had his chin down. The only reason I even attempted was to set up an arm lock, to put his attention on defending his neck, so his arm was left open. I arm-locked him, and he quickly submitted.

Even though it was a pre-planned demonstration, it didn't in any way feel like a simulation to me. When I thumped Goliath back down on the ground—and hard—my heart was pounding with excitement! For me, it felt authentic.

Nevertheless, afterward, Edwardo said jokingly, "was that not a real fight?"

"No, Eduardo, I don't do real fights with big young guys. Well, unless they're new guys who don't know my moves."

A free ebook edition
is available with the
purchase of this book.

To claim your free ebook edition:

Visit MorganJamesBOGO.com
Sign your name CLEARLY in the space
Complete the form and submit a photo of
the entire copyright page
You or your friend can download the ebook
to your preferred device

A **FREE** ebook edition is available for you
or a friend with the purchase of this print book.

CLEARLY SIGN YOUR NAME ABOVE

Instructions to claim your free ebook edition:
1. Visit MorganJamesBOGO.com
2. Sign your name CLEARLY in the space above
3. Complete the form and submit a photo
   of this entire page
4. You or your friend can download the ebook
   to your preferred device

Print & Digital Together Forever.

Snap a photo

Free ebook

Read anywhere

CPSIA information can be obtained
at www.ICGtesting.com
Printed in the USA
JSHW052020160322
23935JS00002B/381